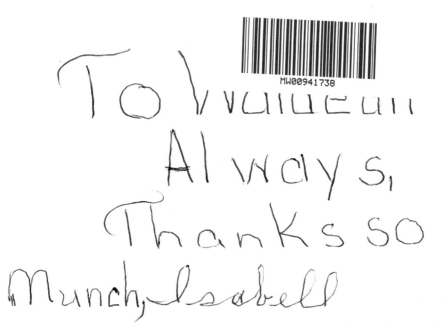

To William
Always,
Thanks so
Munch, Isabell

The Yesteryears

By

Hayward J. Camper

authorHOUSE™

1663 Liberty Drive, Suite 200
Bloomington, Indiana 47403
(800) 839-8640
www.AuthorHouse.com

First published by AuthorHouse 06/27/05

ISBN: 1-4208-2964-5 (sc)
ISBN: 1-4208-5081-4 (dj)

Library of Congress Control Number: 2005902016

Printed in the United States of America
Bloomington, Indiana

This book is printed on acid-free paper.

WASN'T IT JUST YESTERDAY – 50TH ANNIVERSARY

May 23, 1947 – May 23, 1997

Dedicated to my wife, Isabell Josephine Camper

Wasn't it just yesterday we fell in love?
Wasn't it just yesterday we said our vow?
Wasn't it just yesterday I saw the sparkle in your smile?
Wasn't it just yesterday my eyes caught yours and lingered awhile?
Wasn't it just yesterday the joy of living for me begun?
Wasn't it just yesterday the clouds of life gave way for sun?

The calendar says it's fifty years today.
You laugh, smile and came my way.
How can that be?
Oh time! You're going too fast for me.
When all of this life is gone,
Please dear Lord, let it forever be,
This love that is so dear to me,
Not 'til death do us part,
But forever and ever be my heart.

Hayward James Camper

FOREWORD

Hayward J. Camper was born in Newark, New Jersey on November 23, 1919 to educated, professional, loving and caring parents, Archibald and Augusta Camper. The family lived in Baltimore, Maryland until 1925 when they moved to Prescott, Arizona due to Hayward's father's serious health condition. As a World War I veteran, Mr. Camper qualified for a transfer to a government facility in nearby Whipple, Arizona. His doctor believed he would benefit from the warm dry air in the southwest.

At seven years old Hayward went to live with his Aunt Try (Tryphena) in Phoenix, Arizona to attend school. After the death of his mother five years later, Hayward's sister, Blanche and his brother, Douglass were also sent to Phoenix to live with Aunt Try. The three younger siblings remained in Prescott where Hayward's father signed their house over to a man and his wife to stay and take care of his young children. The three younger children later went to a welfare home. Douglass joined his siblings at the welfare home because of friction between him and Aunt Try.

Hayward endured and coped with adversity, shameful verbal and physical abuse, frustration, ridicule and loneliness at school, at home and in every area of his young life. He learned from an early age that privilege came with being white. As a teenager Hayward worked in multiple jobs experiencing and surviving the pain of segregation and discrimination. Notwithstanding the hardships and malicious misfortunes, Hayward kept his eyes on his goal, saved his earnings and maintained his focus. He would go to college someday. He would succeed.

As soon as he was old enough, Hayward thought he would escape to the military. He thought anything would be better than his life in Arizona. What a rude awakening he discovered when he found his adventure in a Mississippi boot camp was worse than any of his previous experiences. He had jumped out of the frying pan into the fire. The disparate treatment of blacks was unimaginable and unconscionable. He was happy to be discharged with a foot disability. However, he never allowed the disappointments of his awful, disdainful and sometimes, discouraging circumstances to thwart his motivation and determination to succeed.

The military GI Bill enabled him to receive a college education. While in college he met and married Isabell J. Dawson and together they attended school and raised their five children. They each eventually received their master's degrees and became teachers and principals in Arizona. Their lives were far from "normal", however.

The excitement of his first principal/teaching job soon turned to fury over racial injustices in the school system of a small northern town in Arizona. He "bucked" the system, questioned their disparate practices and fought for change. The "separate, but equal" policies were separate, but anything but equal and he would not tolerate anything less than equal opportunities for his black students. His trip to the state board of education and persistence resulted in the integration of their high school, but not without consequences to Hayward. He continued to experience discrimination throughout his professional career. Despite the adversities, Hayward persevered and pursued various rewarding positions prior to retiring for the final time in the nineties.

Hayward always wanted to be like his Uncle John who was a medical doctor in general practice back in Maryland. He rationalized that in this profession he could have saved a lot of lives. However, it is my opinion that Hayward probably saved, developed, and impacted more lives while mentoring and teaching young students in: the Navajo Nation Schools, New Mexico Girls School, the various public school systems in Mc Nary, Arizona and Albuquerque, New Mexico, Youth Diagnostic and Development Center, the Heights Psychiatric Hospital, and his volunteer work in various disciplines.

I am amazed at Mr. Camper's resilience. His resolve for justice and equality was not daunted because of his adverse experiences, and he does not appear to be angry, bitter, or to carry a grudge, or harbor any resentment whatsoever. He graciously allows us reminisce vicariously through his personal struggle and quest for justice. His demeanor exudes kindness, gentleness and caring about today's generation of children. He seems even more concerned about doing the right thing today than why things were the way they were.

The following memoirs of Hayward J. Camper represent his life story as he remembers and publicly chronicles his honest opinions. Everything contained in this narrative is from his perspective only and is intended for the personal use of his family members. Therefore, its purpose is not purported as a recording of facts, but rather his world as he observed it at the time. Additionally this account is not intended to be exhaustive, but an attempt to capture significant events in his life.

The content is not necessarily in chronological or any particular order and in some cases it was difficult for him to remember exact dates. The full-page color headshot photo of Mr. and Mrs. Camper was published by permission from Kim Jew Photography Studio, July 9, 2004.

Virginia P. Grant

PART I

CHAPTER 1

The year is 1925 and I am living in Prescott, Arizona with my father (Archibald Hayward Camper), mother (Augusta Viola Camper), sister (Amanda Blanche), brother (Douglass Archibald) and baby sister (Mary Jane). My father had been sent to Arizona by the government for his health since he had contracted tuberculosis while in the army. In those days people felt the dry air of Arizona was better for your health than the humid New Jersey or Maryland air.

My father moved with his family first to Phoenix, Arizona, where he stayed a short time, then he was sent to the government hospital at Whipple, Arizona. The family then moved to Prescott, Arizona to be near him and so he could come home often.

Before being drafted in the military, daddy worked with his mother in the Baltimore public school system. He had never been in the best of health so his mother never thought that he would be drafted into the army. Had she known he would be drafted, she would have presented his medical records to show his condition. Her other two sons, Uncle John Emory and Uncle Douglass were in their last years of medical school. Uncle John was at Howard University in Washington, D.C. and Uncle Douglass was at the University of Pennsylvania Dental School in Philadelphia, Pennsylvania.

Some how the army drafted them, but allowed them to stay in school and complete their education. My two uncles who had always been healthy were able to continue school at government expense. Daddy who had completed school, but always had been sickly was called to active duty in the infantry. It didn't take long for his health to decline and he was discharged and sent back home to Baltimore with a small pension.

My grandmother worked in the Baltimore public school system many years since my grandfather passed away leaving her with three sons and two daughters to raise. One daughter died shortly after my grandfather's death. My grandmother was a strong person, however, and she saw to it that all her children had a good education. She also believed in property ownership. She had property not only in Baltimore, but also around Baltimore. She went to Prescott often to visit her son and his family. There she paid cash for the house daddy lived in and even said she might come to Prescott to live. However, she passed away.

Mother graduated from Hillsdale College in 1917 before marrying daddy. She had intended to teach in the Baltimore city school system, but was in for a complete change when they moved to the west.

I, however, did understand daddy's illness. His tuberculosis seemed to be contagious where he could not teach in any of the public schools in Maryland or Arizona, but he was able to spend some time at home away from the hospital. The times when he came home he worked cleaning offices in town. Mother took in washing to supplement the small pension daddy was getting from the government.

I remember the long clotheslines in the yard, and how I helped to keep the fire going under the tub by adding fuel as necessary to keep the water hot for washing the clothes. We had no hot water tank, but we did have an old Maytag washing machine. It was quite a job getting the clothes washed, rinsed and out on the line. Even today I can see mother hanging and folding clothes. Most people brought their laundry and picked it up. However, for those that lived nearby, I delivered their laundry in a wagon I had gotten for Christmas.

In Baltimore most of the people I came in contact with were black. All the neighbors for blocks around were black families, as I remember. Except for the storekeeper on the corner, I had no contact with white people. Prescott was a different world. There were few black families in town. Those that were living there were usually there because some family member had been sent to the government hospital at Whipple. I soon became aware of segregation. There were eating places in the area, but blacks could not go in them and eat. If a black went to the back door and gave a silly smile, took off his hat, scratched his head, bowed and said please, he could buy something to go. Sometimes mother would take us to the square in the middle of town where we could sit and play on the grass. I remember she used to put a lunch together for us if we were going to be in town for a while. Yes, this was a different world.

Across the street from the square was a barbershop owned by two brothers who were black. They cut white men's hair all day but would not allow a black person in for a haircut. A black person could make arrangements with them to come to the shop at night and they would sneak you in, pull the shades down and you could get a haircut. Segregation was in full bloom. Blacks did go to their public schools because there were so few black children they could not afford to have a separate school for them like they did in the larger Arizona towns. There was no hotel that would accommodate a black person and even the train had a separate car for blacks. Mother sent me on the train to Phoenix several times to visit Aunt Try and I sat in a rail car all by myself. I could not sit in the same car with white people. I thought that was really stupid.

I noticed all this mess though it really didn't bother me. Sometimes it made me feel as if there was something wrong with me and the white race was special. One day it appeared that it was raining in the yard next to ours and we were not getting a drop. A white family lived in that yard and I thought God was giving them rain, watering their grass and flowers because they were white.

In retrospect I feel the treatment black children received during those years destroyed their self-esteem and affected how they valued themselves. Those whose self-esteem were not destroyed were even led to believe some people were better than others and people were not equal. It makes you wonder how black children ever excelled under those conditions. How could a black child experiencing problems approach a white teacher for assistance?

When I was five years old and preparing to go to kindergarten, mother wanted me to get a haircut at the barbershop so I would look nice for school. She had always cut my hair, but for this special occasion she asked daddy to take me since he was home from the hospital. Daddy agreed to take me, but he said he hated going to the shop in Prescott. "I wish we were back in Baltimore where Negro barbers cut blacks' hair in the day during regular business hours and not here where they pull down the shades and sneak you in at night," he told mother. Mother responded that even if every Negro person in Prescott went to their barbershop, they would not earn enough money to support their families. Daddy agreed. There were just no opportunities here for black people. In Baltimore mother could get a teaching position with her college degree and they could hire someone to take care of their children.

"I was talking to a white fellow in the hospital the other day and his wife is teaching with only two years of college and you have a degree and have to take in washing. It's crazy. The government sent me here to live, but is not giving me enough money to take care of my family. Two people with four-year college degrees and you have to take in washing and I have to clean offices." My father was visibly upset as he spoke. "Oh, daddy," she said, we are doing alright."

The next evening daddy took me to the barbershop. They rushed us in, quickly closed the door and pulled down the shades. Daddy asked, "Why do you go through this every time I come here for a haircut? The white people know you are cutting black people's hair after hours."

"Yes, Camper," said one of the barbers. "I know the white folks know, but they don't want black folks in the shop with them and using the same tools to shave them and cut their hair. I had several of them ask me about that. I told them I used another set for blacks because black's hair was not same so I could not use the same tools. Camper, the whites are my bread and butter. I do not intend to lose that trade. There are not enough blacks in Prescott even if every one of them came in for haircuts. The whites are good tippers, too. I have never gotten a tip from a black person. This is the first time this boy has been in for a haircut. Your wife could have brought him in."

"Well," said daddy, you can't expect her to be sneaking around here at night with three children so you can cut the hair of one of them. If I could walk in here in the day like a man for my son to get a haircut, I would tip you, but I don't like sneaking in here and out. I don't feel like tipping."

"I'm sorry, Camper," he said, "I'm doing the best I can in my situation."

Many years later in 1963, the same barbers had a shop in Winslow, Arizona where they were open in the day for anyone who came in. Both daddy and I went to the shop for haircuts and we talked about old times in Prescott.

During this time daddy continued to be in poor health and was living in a nursing home in Winslow. Sometimes there are things you want with all your heart, but you just can't have it. Why were people treating each other the way they did in Prescott? In my mind I was down on the barbers' actions in Prescott, but what could they have done? I now believe that if the Good Lord had made us all the same color, shape, and size we would find some other reason to be different and better than another group of people. I believe if we don't learn to live and work together, we will one day destroy each other, the earth and everything in it.

So how did segregation and that haircut ordeal affect me at the time? I could care less when or if I got a haircut at all. None of that black, white business bothered me at the time. Actually, the sneaking in and pulling the shades down gave me a thrill. The food my mother cooked was better than any food in a restaurant. Riding in an empty rail car to Phoenix never bothered me. The porter always came in and talked to me. I think mother told him to keep an eye on me until I got to Phoenix where Aunt Try was always there to meet me.

My kindergarten year in school was joyful. We lived about a block from school. The first day mother took me and after that I went with an older boy in a higher grade who lived next door. Yes, he was white as was all the other children in my class. I was treated just like all the other children. School was fun. I remember not wanting to go to another grade. I was fearful of changing classes.

But I did enroll in first grade at another school. Daddy or grandmother bought us a house in another part of town. I thought his mother may have bought it or helped him to buy it. She had visited us often. She was in love with the scenery, the mountains, the rocks, the trees and all that nature had to offer. She used to go in the front yard and look up – the sky seemed so close you felt if you were just a bit taller you could reach it. In Baltimore, you opened the front door, you are in the street, open the back door and you are in the alley. Big rats were running up and down the alley as large as cats. There were no mountains, trees, etc. My uncles and their families continued to live there and I wondered how they could. I guess it is what you get used to. Grandmother came to visit and fell in love with the west. I think if she had lived long enough she may have moved out west.

My second year of school was a disaster. Mother went with me the first day to enroll. The school was just a block from where we lived and there were no streets to cross. That would not have been a problem because there was little traffic anyway. After the first day I went to school by myself. Here I am in my eighties and I remember my first day as if it was yesterday. I knew what room to go to because it had been shown to my mother and me on enrollment day.

Remembering my kindergarten experience I knew I was going to enjoy school. I went to the first grade room. It was very attractive with posters and interest centers with fun things for children. Some children were already in the room sitting at a desk and talking to each other. I sat in the next empty desk and tried to talk to the boy sitting next to me, but he got up and moved to another desk. After about five minutes a bell rang and the teacher asked all of us to get up and stand by the chalkboard. She then started calling our names in alphabetical order. The children began to sit in the order their name was called filling the rows of desks. My last name began with a "C" but was not called. I knew she had my name because the day before it had been written with the others. There was one row of desks in the back of the room where no one was sitting. After all the other names were called, she pointed to me and said, "You can sit there," pointing to one of the desks in the empty row in the back. She didn't even call my name. A few of the children laughed. I sat down and wanted to cry. How humiliating.

"What kind of school is this? This isn't like the school I went to in kindergarten. I don't think I'm going to like it," I thought to myself. "Maybe at recess I will find someone to talk to." The children wouldn't talk to me and the teacher seemed angry. I hadn't done anything so I didn't understand why they didn't like me. During recess some of the older children were saying to the children in my class, "Ha ha! You've got a nigger in your class!"

I stayed the entire day, but what a bad day it was. I went home crying and told my mother I did not want to go to that school anymore. I wanted to go to the school I went to last year. She told me we did not live in that part of town now and I had to go to this school. The next day was no better and a few of the older boys threw small rocks at me. As I jumped to avoid the rocks they said, "That's it nigger, dance the jig." Teachers on the playground saw this and did nothing.

I did not go back to class. I ran home and told mother. She told me I had to learn to fight back. I told her I could not fight all of them. She then went back to school with me and was there for a long time talking to people, going to my classroom, talking to my teacher.

Things got a bit better after her visit. I was given a seat with the other children in alphabetical order and the teacher started calling me by my name instead of pointing at me and calling me "You" when talking to me. The teachers on the playground also stopped the rock throwing and some of my classmates even played with me.

Still it was nothing like the kindergarten school. I had the feeling that I was not really wanted. I even once took a dollar from my mother's purse and bought a hundred suckers to pass out to the children so they would like me. That helped for that day, but the next day it was back to the same old, same old.

CHAPTER 2

The winters in Prescott were a mess, snow all the time. How mother managed to do washing the year around, keep house, see about my younger brother and sisters, help with my schoolwork and problems, I will never know. She was a real angel. Maybe that is why God called her home so soon. I remember her telling a cousin who came for a visit that she didn't know what she would do without me. Daddy was not home much, but did the best he could when he was. He cleaned offices at night and went hunting for rabbits and quail for food. Sometimes he took me with him when he went hunting. I enjoyed that, and that meat was oh so good! I have yet to eat any meat that taste as good as those rabbits and quail.

Aunt Try had no children. She had always wanted me to live in Phoenix where she taught the fourth grade at Dunbar Elementary School. This was a school for black children. She had saved my life once when I had pneumonia and a high fever. The doctors said there was no hope for me. I don't remember it but I was told she was at my bed with a towel, which she kept cold by putting it in ice water, wringing out, then putting it on my body. She did this day and night until my fever was gone. What I do remember about that time, however, were little angels flying around the room and asking my mother why all those little people were flying around. That may have been influenced by that high fever.

Hayward J. Camper

My aunt's name was Tryphena (Try-fee-na), but I had a hard time trying to say it so I was told to say Aunt Try. My sisters and brother followed and did the same. Since then I realize that I hear a word right, but when I try to say the word, it does not always come out right.

My parents decided that I would go to Phoenix, live with Aunt Try and go to school there for the third grade. I would come home at holidays and in the summer. I wanted to go, but worried about no one being home to help mother. The next child, my sister, was two years younger than me, and there was a baby brother two years younger than her. I expressed my concerns to my mother. She assured me she would be alright so I went to Phoenix for the third grade.

It was nice going to a school where all the children and staff were black. There were two black elementary schools in Phoenix - Dunbar School where my aunt taught fourth grade and Booker T. Washington school which was only a block from where we lived. I would rather have gone to Booker T. Washington since it was in the neighborhood I lived and most of the children I played with in the evenings and on weekends went to Booker T. Washington. However, my aunt had decided I would go to Dunbar.

The third grade at Dunbar was a dream. I loved it. I wrote mother about once a week. I still remember the address, 107 South Montezuma Street, Prescott, Arizona.

Living in Phoenix was sort of like living in Baltimore in that I had contact with mostly black people, but on a much smaller scale since Phoenix was so much smaller than Baltimore. There were black barbers in the neighborhood cutting the hair of anyone who came in the shop. My only problem was that my aunt kept telling the barber how to cut my hair. That really bothered me. I guessed the barbers hated to see me come to the shop for she would stand by the barber chair and direct every cut. They should have asked her why she didn't keep me home and cut my hair herself, but they didn't. She did this for the first year I was with her. Then she stopped.

10

Aunt Try had a way about herself. She would tell people in a minute what she felt. I remember going to the department store with her to get school clothes. The white clerks acted as if we weren't in the store. They were so busy helping the whites they didn't notice us. I wanted to go and told Aunt Try I would sit outside on the bench and wait for her. She told me no, I would stay in the store. After a time when all the white customers had been served, a clerk came over to get our order. Aunt Try spent no less than 45 minutes walking around with the clerk and having things wrapped. Then she told the clerk he could keep all of it since he didn't want to wait on her in the order she came in. The clerk was really angry and started calling her all kinds of names. I was embarrassed and frightened. We went to another store, got better service and bought the clothes.

After completing the third grade I went back to Prescott for the summer. I could tell my mother was working too hard and told her I wanted to stay in Prescott for the fourth grade so I could be home to help her. She would hear none of that so back to Phoenix I went. I learned that year that some people should do all they can, not to teach a relative. I was in Aunt Try's room for the fourth grade and it was the hardest of all my years of schooling. It was a nightmare. Aunt Try wanted me to be the best student in the class and the more she got after me the worse I got. At the chalk board she would hit me on the head with a piece of chalk and say, "Now get that in your head." The children on the playground started calling me "block head." I later heard that my younger brother had some of the same problems in Aunt Try's classroom. However, Aunt Try failed him. To this day he has not been able to forgive or forget.

In the fourth grade, every Monday there were twenty words on the chalkboard we were to write and study. On Wednesday they were given to us to spell and check our mistakes and study. Then on Friday Aunt Try gave the words to us again. We passed in our papers and she checked them. If we missed over five, we went to the cloakroom, held out our hand and got a lick for every word we missed pass five. This was done for everyone in class. However, sometimes I got a double dose. Aunt Try would start fussing with me at home about my schoolwork and I would have to take my pants

11

down, lay face down on the bed and be whipped with my belt. I was almost a nervous wreck.

Somehow I got to the place where I could spell most of the words on Friday. After practicing and spelling the words correctly on the test, I quickly forgot. If anyone had asked me how to spell them the next day I don't think I would have done well. I had only remembered long enough not to get a whipping! To this day I have always had trouble spelling and pronouncing words. Now, however, I don't feel so bad about it because I can blame poor spelling and pronouncing on old age and not because I'm stupid.

Though, I wrote mother every week telling her I was ready to come and go to the school there, I did not tell her about the whippings, for I didn't want to worry her. I don't remember ever getting a whipping from my mother or father. Of course daddy wasn't home that much, but I don't remember any of us being whipped.

Because of this experience I decided never to have any of my children in a classroom where I was the teacher. However, years later in my first year of teaching, I had both of my daughters in my class. I did not put any more pressure on them than I did on the other students. Now with the new policies, the teacher is to blame for a student's poor work. This was really brought to my attention several years ago when I was doing substitute work. I had a student that did nothing and made no effort. I told him he was getting an "F" from me for that day. He said, "You old fool. You give me an "F", you'll lose your job." Another student spoke up and said, "No, they won't do anything to him, he's just a sub."

Isn't that something? When I went to school and didn't study and do my work it was my fault. Now it is the teacher's, the principal's or anyone at the school, but not the student's fault.

The last of May 1931 I went home to find my mother very sick. Daddy took me to the hospital to see her. She was so sick she didn't know me. She asked my father if I was the doctor. He told her no that it's Hayward.

How could this be? Some how I knew if I was not there to help mother she wouldn't make it. I went to the head of the bed and held her hand. I think she gave me a little squeeze. I thought to myself that I was not going back to Phoenix and I was going to study hard and really be a doctor some day so I could see about her when she got sick. Mother did not get well. She died a couple of days after my hospital visit. God saw she had too much to do and took her home to rest.

When I first went to Phoenix for school I had one sister and one brother. At the time of mother's death I had three sisters and two brothers. That night after mother's death I went outside with them and looking up at the sky, which you could almost touch, I told them that one of the stars was our mother and she was still thinking about us and wanted us to be good so one day we would be up there with her. Mother went to church every Sunday and saw to it that we were at Sunday school and church.

With mother dead daddy really didn't know what to do. His tuberculosis was not active, but he needed to be in the hospital most of the time. It was decided that I would stay with Aunt Try in Phoenix and my older sister and brother would also go to Phoenix and live with her. The two younger sisters and baby brother (only a year old) would stay in Prescott and daddy would give the house to a couple to take care of them. Daddy would then work with the welfare office for the children to go to a welfare home in Phoenix. After a time, a welfare home in Phoenix was found and all my brothers and sisters except the older sister went to the welfare home. My older sister stayed with me at Aunt Try's house.

Aunt Try was a great sister to my father. She told him she would take all of us, but the younger children had heard of her whipping and wanted to stay in the welfare system. My older brother had had enough of Aunt Try. She had failed him in the fourth grade and he wanted out. Aunt Try went to the courthouse and adopted my older sister and me. She wanted me to call her mother. I told her I could never do that. She wasn't too happy, but accepted it. My sister was happy calling her mother.

13

CHAPTER 3

Daddy married the woman in Phoenix who had the welfare home. Why he married her I don't know. She was nothing like my mother. Also, daddy was never home, he was at the hospital most of the time. I guess she thought he wasn't long for this world and he had a $10,000 life insurance policy with the government. That isn't much money but I guess at the time it seemed like a lot. The government was also paying something for each child. Aunt Try never received any money for us unless daddy kept it for the other children.

Once I got out of the fourth grade things went better between Aunt Try and me. I remember the children in the fifth grade saying, "He's not so dumb."

My brother started going to Booker T. Washington Elementary school as soon as he moved into the welfare home. I don't know what the discipline was at Booker T. Washington was, but at Dunbar, whipping was the thing if you didn't get your lessons, got in a fight or were caught smoking at recess behind the school building. Aunt Try was known as a mean teacher. She would take a child to the cloakroom, give a few licks on the hand and think nothing of it. Most of the other teachers would sometimes let things go. If the students got too bad they would be sent to the principal's office where he had a belt and used it for whippings.

I thought my aunt was especially hard on me because she didn't want to show any favoritism. But then, why would she whip me at

14

home? I guess she just really wanted me to be the best. Sometimes she showed a lot of love for both my sister and me.

My sister was a better student than me. She would get in trouble, however, for not eating her breakfast of oatmeal, which she hated. It got to the place where I would eat it to keep her from being in trouble. As we got older privileges were taken away from us if we did something wrong. The worst was to miss my Saturday cowboy movie in town. I really loved those cowboy movies.

I'm sure this happened, but I don't remember it. My brother told me when he was living with Aunt Try I reported him for smoking and he got a whipping. He told me this with anger. He didn't call it a whipping, however, he said a "beating." Maybe that is why I don't remember. I sometimes erase things from my mind that are unpleasant. He could have gotten such a whipping. I told him I was sorry and put it out of my mind.

Aunt Try said smoking would make you weak so I never tried that smoking bit. I enjoyed wrestling at school. I could throw and hold down anyone my size and many of those much larger than me. Once on the playground a little skinny runt decided he wanted to fight me. At recess he was always behind the school building smoking so I figured I would have no trouble beating his behind, even it I had to go to the principal's office for a whipping. I tore into that boy thinking I would beat him before recess was over and then go to class as if nothing had happened. To my surprise he was as strong as an ox. Neither one of us heard the bell ending recess so both of us ended up in the principal's office. I would say the fight was a draw. I don't know what he would say, but he never again decided to fight me.

After the fight, I thought my aunt may not know what she was talking about, but I still did not try smoking until many years afterwards. I was in a government hospital during World War II waiting for the doctors to decide if they should operate on my foot for a problem or discharge me. My army buddies told me if I smoke it would make the time pass quickly. I got a carton and started smoking away. It

15

wasn't long before I was so sick, I thought I was going to die. I never tried it again.

One of my summers was a living hell. Uncle Douglass never did like the idea of his sister taking on the responsibility of his brother's children. One summer before my grandmother's death, Aunt Try took me to Philadelphia to visit my uncle. He's the one who graduated from the University of Pennsylvania with a degree in dentistry. His home and dental office were in Philadelphia. He later gave up his practice and moved to Baltimore to teach. This seemed like a stupid move to me, but I never heard why he did it. I don't remember how old I was, but I was still in elementary school.

Uncle Douglass said if I was not tired enough when I went to bed, I would play with myself until I went to sleep. To be sure I was tired enough, he made me go to the square that was across the street from the house and run around it until I was tired then come back to the house and go to bed. If I was older, I never would have allowed this to happen to me. There were trees in the square that had caterpillars living on them. Some of them fell on me and bit me. I would immediately start itching when I got in bed and start scratching. My uncle would say I was playing with myself, come in with a belt, and start beating me, yelling, "Keep your hands above your head and stop playing with yourself." Grandmother was visiting once when this happened. She came into the room hollering for him to stop.

This is just one example of his strange actions. The man was crazy. He found any reason to beat me. Aunt Try would say nothing as if I needed a man's disciplining. Many, many years later he came to Albuquerque where I was living at that time to visit his brother (my father) who was in a nursing home and he told me he was sorry for the way he had treated me. I was shocked that nearly seventy years had passed, both of us old men now, and he remembered and brought it up. "Oh Uncle," I said, "That was long ago. Let's forget it." Though I said this, it was something neither one of us could forget.

While in grade school I sold newspapers on weekends. Aunt Try gave both my sister and me spending money, but I liked making money on my own. When I got older I started working weekends and in the summer for a man who was a friend of Aunt Try. He owned and operated a wood, sand and gravel yard. He also went to a watermelon field in the summer where we picked melons and loaded them on a truck for delivery to stores in town. The melon picking was fun. We would get hot and thirsty in the hot summer heat, then "bust" a melon to eat.

The heat in Phoenix was something to reckon with. We didn't have air conditioning like there is today. Aunt Try would place a block of ice in a tub and have an electric fan blow over it to cool the room. When I was selling papers I would spend most of my profit drinking five-cent bottles of soda pop.

My worst summer job was loading trucks with cow manure from the Phoenix stock yards and loading it on railroad cars. We had no protection for our face and dust would get into my lungs. I was in real misery. I didn't have to go with the men on the stock yard jobs, but I was a young teen and wanted to show I could do as much work as any man. I was also saving money for college. I knew Aunt Try would help me once I was in college, but I wanted to help myself as much as I could. I enjoyed working, showing the men I could loan a truck with sand and gravel as quick or quicker than any of them.

I guess it was not easy for Aunt Try being a single parent with two children, living on a teacher's salary. One day I overheard her telling some friends of hers, "My brother never sends me anything for his children." She liked relaxing on weekends by having her friends over to play cards and talk. They were always laughing and talking and I never really paid any attention to them or what they said. But, this time those words caught my ear. I got so angry I wanted to rush into the room and say something to her, but decided to wait until her company left.

Daddy was now living with his family in San Diego. He had gotten a transfer to a government hospital in California. I had just completed the seventh grade. It was summer and I was working at

17

the wood yard. I had saved a little money in a savings account in the bank. I asked Aunt Try how she expected daddy to send her any money for us when he only had a small government pension, and his other children were using surplus commodities to live on. I told her she could have the money I had in the bank, and for her to add up everything she had spent on me, and once I had finished medical school, started working I would pay her back every cent.

My aunt was in shock. "Oh Hayward!" She said, "I am sorry you heard me. I was just talking. I don't expect anything from your father." This wasn't good enough for me. I said nothing but decided to leave and go to San Diego where my brothers and sisters were living. That night when everyone was asleep, I packed a few things in a bag and was on my way to San Diego.

We lived near the railroad tracks and I had in mind to get on a freight car, but I didn't know where it would go so I figured my best bet was to hitchhike and stay on the highway where there were signs to show where the road was going. Hitchhiking was rough. Several drivers tried to have sex with me. One car was almost wrecked as I struggled with one of the drivers to stop the car and let me out. I had money in the bank. I should have cooled down, taken it out and bought a bus ticket, but no, like an angry fool, I just took off. Well, it's lucky I wasn't killed. After about five days on the road I finally got to San Diego.

Daddy's wife was glad to see me. She and Aunt Try never did like each other and when living in Phoenix they had some angry words when they met. It didn't help matters that my brother had left Aunt Try's house and told Miss. Barber how Aunt Try had treated him, and that she had failed him in the fourth grade. My brother called her mother. I could never do that. Barbara was her first name but I called her Miss. Barber and she accepted me using that name. I could not even bring myself to call her Mrs. Camper.

When they lived in Phoenix I would go by to see my brothers and sisters, but I did not tell Aunt Try about my visits because she had told me to stay away from their house. Now Miss Barber had something to throw into my aunt's face. I had run away from my aunt to live with her.

Miss Barber took me to the second-hand store and bought me clothes. She then took me to San Diego Memorial Junior High to enroll me in school. It looked like things were going to be all right. Miss Barbara was a missionary woman and on Sundays, she went to church dressed in white. She also had people coming to the house for prayer meetings.

My second Sunday there, I went to church with her and my brothers and sisters. She had a special place she sat with some other women all in white. She had us sit on a bench near the front. During the service she would jump up and shout until some men would grab her and hold her down and one of the sisters would fan her with one of their fans. She did this several times. I thought, what have I gotten myself into? I should have stayed home. Then she got up and pointed to where we were sitting, shouting and dancing she said, "Look at them! Those poor motherless children with their father in the veteran's hospital and me doing all I can to take care of them. The extra one I told you about is here today. Any help you can give, the Lord will surely bless you. Please find it in your heart to help."

Well, that did it. I wanted to drop dead. Never, in my life had anything this awful happened to me. I jumped up and ran out of church crying all the way home. The first thing I thought of was going back to Phoenix, but I had just left there. I would feel like a fool going back.

Miss Barber came home so angry, she shook me and asked what was wrong with me running out of church like that. She told me I wasn't with my school teaching aunt anymore and my father's pension was near nothing. She had to use surplus commodities, public assistance and all the help from the Lord she could get to take care of us. She would never take me to church again.

I almost did it – I almost ran out of the house, got back on the road and to Phoenix. But since I just left there I couldn't do it.

Memorial Junior High was a real plus for me. In San Diego all the children went to school together. It differed from Prescott in that they even had some black teachers there and all the children were treated with respect. Teachers were teaching subjects that were their major or minor in college. No one made fun of me or threw rocks at me. The school had a nice library, science equipment, home economics, physical education and shop. This was wonderful. I could stay here for school, finish high school and go to the University of California for medical school. I just had to make it work.

I got jobs for weekends and evenings. With the nice weather in San Diego people had green yards all year so I was able to get plenty of yard work. The people I worked for were very nice to me. If the weather was hot they would bring me a cool drink and suggest I rest a while. If it was their mealtime they would invite me in to eat. Hearing of my plans to stay in school they did all they could to encourage me. Here were white people like the people I had in Prescott at my kindergarten school.

I could have lived with several of the families I worked for and gone to school. I know it is wrong to let your home business out, but I was so miserable and some of the families were so nice, I just let it out. They told me that my working around the house and in the yard would more than make up for my room and board. I almost did it.

What a nice town, wonderful school – why couldn't I have a good home life? Things at home were really a mess. Miss Barbara always had the house filled with people praying and she was telling them how poor we were and thanking them for their help.

I decided to stay the year, graduate from junior high then go back to Phoenix for school. I put some of the money I made from yard work into a savings account, and I also gave Miss Barber some trying to have some kind of peace with her. I didn't let her know about my bank savings account. I let her think what I was spending foolishly. I bought little things for my brothers and sisters and sometimes something for the house.

The house had a basement where my brothers, sisters and I had our beds. Miss Barber hardly came down there so I could get things and keep them there without her knowledge. She didn't really care, the upper part of the house was available for her religious activity. Her son, several years older then me had a room in the upper part of the house. I never cared for him. Daddy was never home the whole time I was there. He was in the hospital in Los Angeles.

I graduated from junior high school, took my money out of the bank and took a bus back to Phoenix. I didn't tell my aunt I was coming back. However, I had made arrangements with one of the families in San Diego that if things didn't work out in Phoenix I would come back and stay with them.

CHAPTER 4

Once I got to Phoenix I didn't feel good about coming back, considering the way I left. I almost got back on the bus to go back to San Diego. With my head down, I went into the house, said hello to Aunt Try, told her I had graduated from junior high, and asked if it was all right for me to stay with her and go to high school. She said, of course I could stay and something about I never should have left. She had known something about the way Miss Barber lived when she was in Phoenix and perhaps she figured I may be back.

There I was, back in the world of segregation. I went back to the wood yard to work for the summer and weekends once school started. I continued depositing money into my savings account, thinking about college.

Carver High School was really a step down in education. It wasn't the staff's fault. They did the best with what they had. Phoenix had a nice high school with a campus that looked like a college, but I couldn't go there. I wondered how I could be living in the same country, in a state next to and not many miles away from California with people and customs so different. It brought to my mind when I was at Dunbar School and the song, "Am I Blue?" came out. The children at recess on the playground would joke around singing, "Am I Blue." Then someone would start laughing and holler out, "No You're Black!" At times some boy would try to get the attention of some "light skin" girl and some one would say, "You are crazy man. The blacker the berry, the sweeter the juice."

Carver High campus was like a small elementary school. The principal spent part of his day teaching. Most teachers had as many as three subjects to teach and some of them were teaching subjects they did not take in college so they had to study along with their class. The courts said, separate but equal, but we all knew better. It was not even close. And, it was not just Arizona, but many other states were in the same situation. Yet even with this handicap, many black children were going on to college and becoming successful in their occupations.

I graduated from Carver High School, May 1938. Because of my work in the wood yard, I had saved about two thousand dollars. I still wanted to be a medical doctor. One of my uncle's was practicing medicine in Baltimore, was an outstanding person in the community, and gave of his time to some people who could not afford a doctor. I always did admire him and wanted to do the same.

I knew I could get help from Aunt Try for college and medical school, but since I had acted a fool and moved out, then came back, I wasn't about to ask for any help from her.

I decided I would go to Baltimore for the summer, work until about three weeks before school started, then go to Washington, get an evening job and be ready to enroll in Howard University. When my uncle went to Howard he played on their football team and did very well. I played football at Carver, did well, and enjoyed it. I wasn't sure I would be able to play for Howard and work too, but it was in the back of my mind.

I decided since my uncle who was teaching school in Baltimore, had a small family (two children) and living rent free in a large house belonging to my aunt, I would stay with him. My other uncle had a large house, but he had six children and his medical office was also in the house. His wife was also operating a hair dressing business there.

23

I could tell my uncle wasn't too happy to have me. He and his sister were very close and he let her know she should have let his brother keep all his children even if they had to be in welfare homes.

I had been in Baltimore about a month, had a job and was looking forward to the fall when I would move to Washington, D.C. and enroll at Howard University. I received my first check (I don't remember how much it was) and my uncle surprised me by saying I would have to pay something for room and board. I told him I would not be there long and I was saving for college. He told me that did not matter I would have to pay for time I was there or get out.

I was very angry and asked him why should I have to pay and he wasn't paying anything to my aunt for living there. That did it. I had to move out that day. I gathered my things and went to the other uncle's house. He said I could stay with them as long as I wanted and not worry about paying anything. I thought about it for a while then decided I would go back to California. Daddy was in a soldier's home near Los Angeles. He had divorced Miss Barber who was still living in San Diego with her son. My brothers and sisters were in a welfare home in Los Angeles.

California had been good for me when I lived in San Diego. I could get a job and go to the University of California. I contacted my father and he made arrangements for me to rent a room from a family in Los Angeles.

Soon after I got to Los Angeles I went to the employment office to find a job. They had many jobs listed but I wanted something where I could go to school and have time to study. There was a job listed in Westwood for room and board and the salary was open. I went to see about it. There was a nice large room and bath over the garage. The family included a man, his wife and two sons. The husband was a sound director for one of the movie companies. They wanted a house boy to take care of the yard and help in the house with the cleaning.

I made up my mind to take the job and go to Los Angeles Junior College for two years then transfer to the university. I would only need money for books and transportation, which the family said they would take care of and pay me $3.00 a week. The weeks that school was not in session, I would be paid a little more. This arrangement was very nice – like a dream come true. I ate breakfast with the family and the mother fixed a lunch for me as she did for her husband and her sons to carry to school. The family paid for my pass on the bus to school. They also paid for my college tuition. When I came home from school I helped with the supper dishes and cleaning of the kitchen, then the rest of the time was mine. I knew it, California was the place for me.

I enrolled in Junior college. Some weekends I visited my brothers and sisters in town or daddy at the Soldier's Home to play checkers with him. Other times if there was a lot of yard work or things that needed done I just stayed home and did my chores.

Hayward J. Camper

my mother

left: my grandmother, approx. 1925
right: my mother & Mary Jane (sister), approx. 1925

PIN PRESENTED — Erling E. Anderson, Guidance Supervisor at Greasewood Boarding School, receives a 30-year pin from Ernest Magnuson, Education Superintendent. Bureau of Indian Affairs. Ft. Defiance Agency. Presentation was in recognition of his continuous service to the Bureau. Seated are Mrs. Anderson and Greasewood principal Hayward Camper.

top left: Brother - Douglass; Prescott, AZ; Feb. 8, 1924
top right: Me, Blanche and Douglass; Feb. 9, 1924

top: Prescott, Arizona; 1920's
bottom: Baltimore; May 1921

top: Baltimore, Maryland
bottom: Hayward - August, 1922

1924 my father, sister and me
Granite Dells, Arizona

Blanche - 1922

Whipple

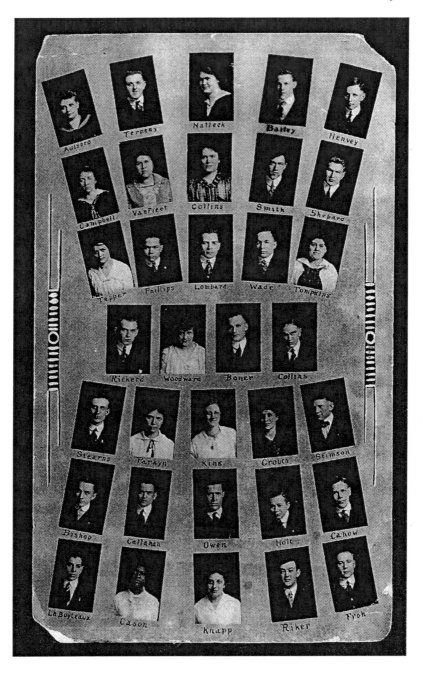

My Mother
1917 Graduation Class
Hillsdale College

The United States of America

honors the memory of

ARCHIBALD H. CAMPER

This certificate is awarded by a grateful nation in recognition of devoted and selfless consecration to the service of our country in the Armed Forces of the United States.

Ronald Reagan

President of the United States

Hillsdale College History

Hillsdale College, founded by Freewill Baptists as Michigan Central College in Spring Arbor, Michigan, began classes in December of 1844. The college later moved to Hillsdale, Michigan in 1853 and assumed its current name. As stated in the Preamble to its Articles of Incorporation, the College undertakes its work "... grateful to God for the inestimable blessings resulting from the prevalence of civil and religious liberty and intelligent piety in the land, and believing that the diffusion of sound learning is essential to the perpetuity of these blessings..."

Though it was established by Freewill Baptists, the College has been officially non-denominational since its inception. Like the American Founders, the College emphasizes the importance of the common moral truths that bind all Americans, while recognizing the importance of religion for the maintenance of a free society.

One of only 119 American colleges awarding four-year liberal arts degrees in 1850, Hillsdale was the first American college to prohibit in its charter all discrimination based on race, religion, or sex. That is, Hillsdale was the first American college to be chartered on the principle of nondiscrimination. Hillsdale's Founders shared a devotion to the principle of equality with the Founders of America who had declared in 1776 that "all men are created equal."

Because of its dedication to the principle of equality, Hillsdale became an early force for the abolition of slavery and for the education of black students; in fact, blacks were admitted immediately after the 1844 founding. The College became the second in the nation to grant four-year liberal arts degrees to women.

Leading orator and itinerant preacher Ransom Dunn, who would serve the College in leadership roles for half a century, raised money to construct the new hilltop college in Hillsdale during the early 1850s by riding 6,000 miles on horseback and preaching for two years on the Wisconsin and Minnesota frontier.

Personal tragedies marked his life-including his own poor health, weak eyesight, and the deaths of his wife, three infant daughters, a son in the Civil War, and an older son. Yet, during the half century after 1850, Professor Dunn courageously secured the foundation of Hillsdale College. Hillsdale College would survive while over 80% of colleges founded before the Civil War would fail.

The Hillsdale tradition did not emerge in a vacuum but was forged in the crucible of history. A higher percentage of her young men enlisted in the Civil War than from any other western college. Of the more than 400 men serving

half became officers. During the conflict, four Hillsdale students won the
Congressional Medal of Honor, three became generals, and many more
served as regimental commanders. Sixty died.

Because of its early crusade against slavery, 'ts role in helping to found the
Republican party in Jackson in 1854 (President Edmund Fairfield was a leading
founder of the party), and its location on the first railroad to pass through
Michigan to Chicago, Hillsdale College was a natural site for more than two
dozen nationally recognized speakers in the antebellum and Civil War eras.

A short list of the prominent speakers includes Frederick Douglass, Edward
Everett - who spoke before Lincoln at Gettysburg and gave his library to
Hillsdale College while President of Harvard, Governor Austin Blair who also
served on the Hillsdale faculty, Senator Zachariah Chandler, Senator Charles
Sumner, Carl Schurz, Wendell Phillips, Senator Lyman Trumbull, Owen
Lovejoy, and William Lloyd Garrison.

An authority on higher education in the American West recently placed ten
Hillsdale students on his short list of the fifteen most outstanding graduates
from all Michigan colleges in the nineteenth century. Hillsdale was one of two
colleges west of the Appalachians with the highest percentage of alumni listed
in the first Who's Who in America.

So it was that Hillsdale graduates reflected the college motto: Virtus
Tentamine Gaudet (Virtue rejoices in doing). In 1891 the Chicago Herald
reported that Hillsdale College was second in standing to no denominational
college in the country. Hillsdale even declined a formal proposal to unify with
the University of Chicago in 1895.

Hillsdale continued to overcome many obstacles in the 20th century. In the
1930s and 1940s the college faced the near foreclosure of mortgages. In the
1970s, some of its students were receiving federal loans which the
government used as a pretext for interference with the College's internal
affairs.

Hillsdale's trustees responded with two toughly-worded resolutions: One, the
College would continue its policy of non-discrimination. Two, the College, "with
the help of God," would "resist, by all legal means, any encroachments on its
independence."

In 1979, this continuing battle with the Department of Health, Education, and
Welfare (HEW) began to intensify. The College filed a petition for judicial
review in the Sixth Circuit Court of Appeals in Cincinnati, asking the court to
overturn a previous decision by the Reviewing Authority, Office of Civil Rights
of HEW. This decision would have required Hillsdale to submit Assurance of
Compliance forms mandated by Title IX as a condition of the continued receipt
of federal financial assistance by two hundred Hillsdale students.

Hillsdale's petition was based in part upon tradition - the pioneering College
had a tradition of graduating women, blacks, and other minorities since before
the Civil War. In December 1982, the Sixth Circuit Court of Appeals vindicated
Hillsdale's refusal to sign the compliance forms, but it also ruled that
government aid to individual students could be terminated without a finding
that a college actually discriminated. Hillsdale subsequently announced that it
was carrying this battle for educational freedom to the highest American court.

In February 1984 in a related case, Grove City College v. T.H. Bell, Secretary

U.S. Department of Education, the U. S. Supreme Court made a decision regarding arguments first made by Hillsdale College. It required every college or university to fulfill federal requirements because its students received federal aid.

Because Hillsdale under the Grove City College decision would have had to sign compliance forms to protect students formerly on government aid, the College instead successfully generated an additional $1,000,000 annually from private sources. Today, the college turns down federal taxpayer money to the tune of $5 million per year, which it replaces entirely with private contributions.

Due in no small part to its courageous stand, the College raised enough extra revenue to pay the equivalent of the federal loans that it would now refuse. The Detroit Free Press on January 25, 1981 stated, "Hillsdale after all, is famous as the little college that fights for rightness and independence. From the unlikely location of south central Michigan, it gained its national recognition by drawing its sword against the federal government. No trespassing, it told HEW; we'll hire, promote, subsidize, educate and influence with no interference from you."

Hillsdale College continues to carry out its mission today as it has every year since 1844. It teaches its students the skills to be productive citizens and the moral virtues to be good ones. Today this small college continues to "go it alone," to do things its own way, even when that way is neither profitable nor popular, but right.

A prayer written in the Bible that was placed inside the 1853 cornerstone reflects a continuing commitment of one and a half centuries: "May earth be better and heaven be richer because of the life and labor of Hillsdale College."

Honorable Discharge from The United States Army

TO ALL WHOM IT MAY CONCERN:

This is to Certify, That * *Archibald H. Camper.*

† *3005733 Private Co E Dev Bn*

THE UNITED STATES ARMY, *as a* TESTIMONIAL OF HONEST AND FAITHFUL

SERVICE. *is hereby* HONORABLY DISCHARGED *from the military service of the*

UNITED STATES *by reason of service in longer require set forth*
in letter T.O. Nov 19, 1918 Hq. Camp Humphreys, a Feb 3, 1919
Said Archibald H. Camper . . . . . *was born*

in Baltimore . . . . , *in the State of Maryland*

When enlisted he was 2 7 years of age and by occupation a Teacher

He had black eyes, dar coie hair, black complexion, and

was 5 feet 7 ½ inches in height.

Given under my hand at Camp's AA Humphreys this

2 d day of . . . one thousand nine hundred and nineteen

John C Zimarch

Major Eug Ill'A
Commanding.

Form No. 526, A. G. O.
Oct. 9-18.

* Insert name, Christian name first . e. g. "John Doe."
† Insert Army serial number, grade, company and regiment or arm or corps or department; e. g., "1,630,300"; "Corporal,
Company A, 1st Infantry"; "Sergeant, Quartermaster Corps"; "Sergeant, First Class, Medical Department."
‡ If discharged prior to expiration of service, give number, date, and source of order or full description of authority therefor.

PART II

CHAPTER 5

In 1938 I enrolled at Los Angeles City College for the fall semester of pre-med. My high school had not prepared me for college. If I had stayed in the California school system and graduated from one of their high schools I would have been ready for one of their universities. I was determined to make it. I studied late into the night and cut my visits to my brothers, sisters and father to once a month.

I stayed the course through the spring semester of 1940, then with low grades and the feeling of little progress I dropped out of school and took a job in the shipyard. The pay was good and I was seeing a girl who had one son and a child on the way, which she said was mine. Her mother wanted us to get married. Now that I was not going to school and had a good job I considered. A number of my classmates who graduated with me had married and had families. I wanted a family and I loved the girl I was dating and her son. She was a bit on the wild side, however. She did a lot of going out and riding with other men in their cars. She lived in a house that was very crowded with her mother and sister. Her sister also had a child and wasn't married. Men were in and out of the house constantly. I didn't have a car and didn't know how to drive. This girl and her son would be too much for me. I wanted to move on, but then she was saying the child she was carrying was mine and I had been helping her with her son. I shuddered to think of her alone with another child to take care of.

I told her mother that her daughter was too wild for me. Her mother said once her daughter got married she would settle down. She would move into the apartment I was living in and be busy keeping house. This is what I wanted to happen, so I believed it would happen.

Her mother drove us to Yuma, Arizona to get married. There was a waiting period in California, which I was prepared for, but her mother thought I might change my mind or run away. I got married. "Oh what fools we mortals be."

Once we were married everything changed. My wife refused to move in the apartment with me. She said she wanted to wait until the baby was born to move and she wanted a house to live in not an apartment. This I thought was crazy. She lived in a house now, but it only had two small bedrooms, was very crowded, and was smaller than my apartment. I tried staying over in her mother's house, but it was such a mess I went back to my apartment.

The baby was born, a baby girl. I told my wife we had to move out of her mother's house. It was too crowded. I even got another shipyard job to hurry the time so I could buy a house. The shipyards were all in the same area so I completed my shift at one then walked to the other and started another shift.

The baby girl got sick. I told my wife it was too crowded for her. She still wouldn't move. Then the baby died. That did it for me. With the baby dead and my wife refusing to move in with me even though I had enough money for a down payment on a house, I decided to get away from it all. I went to the recruitment office and enlisted in the military. They told me I was eligible for Officers' training school since I had two years' of college. I would do basic training in California then I would be sent to an officer's training school with the infantry.

CHAPTER 6

I had a tumor on my right foot that had been operated on twice as a child, but it came back each time. The foot never really gave me any trouble, but with all the marching and drilling it started swelling and I had a noticeable limp. I was examined and told I would not be able to be an officer in the infantry because of my foot and that was the only department they had black officers except in the medical department and I would have had to completed my medical education to be considered for that.

I was reclassified as limited service and sent to Camp Van Dorn, Mississippi. What a change. What a surprise! Nothing had prepared me for this. It was like being in another country.

Our company was in the middle of a large area surrounded by other companies that were white. Most of the men in my company were from the south and on limited service because they could not read or write. At first the army would not take them because of this handicap. However, as the war continued and more white men went into service and the white women started going out with black men the government saw they had to do something or had a lot of intermarriage. They took these men into the army to do the work of laborers. You did not have to know how to read or write to do the jobs they did. The company did have some college degree black officers. I don't know their classification. I was put to work on hospital duty with some other soldiers in my company, cleaning, emptying bed pans, etc.

There was a common dining hall and infirmary. The soldiers in the white company ate first then the soldiers from the black company would come in to eat. The dining area was always a mess when we went to eat. Sometimes all the meat or dessert would be gone and sometimes both were gone. This really disturbed me. How could a government be so stupid to treat its soldiers like this? In the infirmary whites were taken care of first, and unless you had visual signs of a broken bone, bleeding, or were unconscious, the doctor would tell you, "There is nothing wrong with you that a little work won't cure."

Can you believe this? A war is going on and we're in the army fighting for our country and being treated like shit! The black companies received their rifle and ammunition to practice at the rifle range and turned them in when they returned to the barracks. The white companies carried their rifle and ammunition back to the barracks with them.

One day a group of us went to the camp commander and asked for better treatment. Before we got too far we found ourselves surrounded by white soldiers with machine guns mounted on army trucks. Next a car drove up with one of the black officers from our company in it. I was so angry at the time I didn't care if I was shot. I asked the black officer how in the hell they expected to win a war treating some of their soldiers like this. I was told to keep my damn mouth shut and go back to my barracks or I would find myself in the guardhouse with a dishonorable discharge. I went back to the barracks.

Being in the army in California was nice but this was like a different army. Why couldn't we all be treated the same? I wondered if the people in Washington knew what was going on. Well, I thought I'd better make the best of it. Maybe I will not have to be here for a long time and I will be moved someplace else. Any place will be better than here.

Well, Washington took care of my problem. An order came out saying there would be no more limited service. Examine all your limited service men. Correct what causes them to be classified limited service or discharge them. I don't know what happened to the men who could not read or write, but I was put in the hospital and told they were going to operate on my foot. They asked me if that would be all right and I told them it would. The next day I was told that since I had had my foot operated on twice before, the doctors thought it best to discharge me. On October 12, 1943 I received an honorable discharge from the army.

In a system that isn't fair in the first place one can work in it to do the best they can or cry and do nothing or even let it destroy you. Here I was crying about the system and could have been shot, or given a less than honorable discharge. Thank God for the new law that prohibited limited service. It was full duty or no duty and for me it was no duty.

I looked back and wondered what I was thinking of. I went back to Los Angeles. I moved in with my wife at her mother's house and got a job cleaning a Sherman Doughnut Shop. I worked there until I could find something better and then I would try again to move my family.

It was around this time that the G.I. Bill was passed. Uncle Sam would give me money for my family to live on and pay all my college expenses for a year plus my army time. If when the time ran out I was half way through a semester, they would see me through. That would be a year plus sixteen months for me. I could work cleaning the doughnut shop in the evening and have the day free for school.

I told my wife and her mother what I wanted to do. They said I was crazy. I had two years of college and the best I had now was cleaning a doughnut shop, even Uncle Sam didn't want me. I didn't know what to do. Another child had been born, a boy. I knew leaving my wife with three children to take care wasn't the right thing to do. I tried to show my wife and her mother that the family would be well taken care of. It wasn't as if I was going to stop working. We would really have more money coming in than we had now. In time we have our own place.

Why I couldn't make them understand, I don't know. It seemed as if the mother didn't really want her daughter to leave even though at one time she said it was alright. Well, I wasn't going to stay around and try to figure it out.

I was really tired of all the men in and out of the house and my wife going riding with them and thinking nothing of it. Coming back to Los Angeles may have been the right thing to do, but moving in with my wife in her mother's house was a mistake. I thought about staying in Los Angeles, but getting a place of my own to live and go to school. I already had a job and with the G.I. bill I could enroll in the University of California. But would I be able to stay away from my wife and her family? Perhaps not. I decided to be "born again." Start my life (which had been a mess) over again. I would go some place where I knew no one and no one knew me. I had three places in mind: Flagstaff, Arizona; Albuquerque, New Mexico; and Denver, Colorado.

I packed my bags and got a greyhound bus to Flagstaff. I had no trouble getting a job at the Monte Vista Hotel as a bellhop, working from 3:00 PM to 11:00 PM. This was perfect. I had most of the day for classes and the night for sleeping. I decided to forget about medical school since my G,I, Bill would run out before I could complete medical school. In retrospect I look back and think that with working and going to school with the help from the government, I could have come to Albuquerque for medical school and made it. I don't think we come this way again, but if I do, I'll make it next time!

I don't remember what my salary was but what I didn't get in pay I more than made up for in tips. The hours I worked were a good time to catch travelers coming in for the night. The hotel had three floors and it was my job to use the elevator to take guests to their room and answer questions they had. I had a platform near the elevator in the lobby where I did my schoolwork. Most people wanted to know what I was doing and once they found out I was a G.I. going to school on the G.I. Bill they would give me a large tip. Deep down, at times, I did not feel good about this. I felt like I was begging, but then I told myself it wouldn't be like this for long. I never did what another fellow did that worked there. The guest gave him a dime and he gave it back saying, "You need it worse than I do." A few times a guest would not have any change and say, "Thank you." I would say, "You're welcome." I was just as polite with that person as any other guest.

I enrolled in Arizona State College at Flagstaff in September 1944 and graduated in 1947 with a major in education and mathematics and a minor in physical science and English. I don't know how I got a minor in English. It seemed that from the fourth grade on I have had trouble with the English language. In college I was always taking an English course for some deficiency. The college students called it "bone head" English. One reason for my mathematics major was numbers in place of words.

Could it be that what happened to me in Aunt Try's fourth grade room years ago has followed me the rest of my life, or am I using that as an excuse for being a poor reader and speller? I know my aunt wanted the best for me and would never knowingly do anything to hurt me. Even the many whippings were to make my future brighter and maybe they did.

This was a good time to enroll in college. All of the schools were going all out to attract veterans. The college accepted me with open arms as did the town. Many movies were made in the area and often we had guests from California working on a picture. They always left me a very big tip when they checked out of the hotel. If they checked out in the day when I was not on duty, they would leave it with the hotel clerk. I was making more money than I made working two shipyard jobs in California.

Flagstaff, Arizona wasn't California and the town had strange ways about it that I accepted and went on with my life. The manager was serving in the Navy when I was hired. His wife hired me and was very nice seeing to it my working hours did not interfere with my schoolwork. She encouraged me. When her husband came back from service he did the same. However, porter, cook or dishwasher were the only jobs allowed me in the hotel. I could go to the hotel restaurant and get food for the guest, carry it to their room, but I could not go to the restaurant and order and sit down to eat. This really didn't bother me. I hardly even thought about it. I wanted an education and that is what I was getting.

CHAPTER 7

I was in Flagstaff about six months when I received word my wife had been killed in a car accident. She liked to go riding and most of the time the children stayed with her mother. I guess I would have had a better hold on her if I had bought a car, but at the time I never thought of it.

With my wife dead her mother wanted me to send money to her for the children. I thought if I was going to send money and be responsible for the three boys I would bring them to Arizona to be with me. I never did care for the type of people that were in and out of my mother-in-law's house. I had been staying in a room I rented, but now that the children may be coming I rented a house and asked my sister who lived in Phoenix to come to Flagstaff and stay a while to help me with the boys.

My mother-in-law took the case to court. The judge asked me how I was going to work, go to school and take care of three boys, one who was just a baby. I told him about the house and my sister. He told me to take the boys. I picked up one boy and took the hand of the other boy who was holding his brother's hand and started walking out of the courthouse. My mother-in-law started screaming, "Judge, they're not his!"

The judge asked me to stop. I turned around and came back. The judge asked her what did she mean saying the children weren't his. She said she meant the older one wasn't mine. The judge told the older boy to go to his grandmother and for me to take the other two. Then with one boy in my arms and holding the hand of the other boy I walked out of the courtroom. The grandmother ran behind me crying, "Please, don't take my babies."

I felt sorry for her and I almost gave in to her crying, but I knew because of the company she kept, her daughter never had a chance to live a happy and useful life. I did not care who was the father of the boys, their mother was dead and they needed someone to take care of them and given the opportunity I was going to do it.

My sister stayed in Flagstaff a few months then went back to Phoenix. I found a nice family for my boys to stay with. That arrangement worked well. Flagstaff, like some other small towns in Arizona in 1946 had three separate educational systems for grades one through eight – one for Hispanics, one for whites and one for blacks. For high school, grades nine through twelve every one went to school together, but all the teachers at the high school were white.

I was in my senior year in college and ready to do my practice teaching for my secondary teaching certificate. I was told I would have to do it at the black elementary school in their upper grades. I questioned this. If I was studying to teach in a high school why not do my practice teaching in a regular high school? My advisor told me working with the seventh and eighth grades at the elementary school would still qualify me for a secondary certificate. I told my college advisor that may be so, but I wanted to teach in a regular high school and felt I should have the opportunity to do my practice teaching in one. My advisor told me that would be the best thing to do, but no black teacher graduating from the college, whether elementary or secondary did their practice teaching in a white school. He said he would check into it.

After about a week the advisor told me I was to meet with the school superintendent, principal, and several of the math and science teachers I would be working with at Flagstaff High School. He gave me the date and time. Boy! Now I wasn't sure I wanted to do it. Then I thought, what the heck! If they turn me down I could just go to the black elementary school.

That meeting at the high school went well. They wanted to know why I wanted to do my practice teaching there, and if it caused a problem with parents would I be willing to transfer to the black school. I responded that I did not want to create any problems for them, and if there were problems I would transfer.

My practice teaching at Flagstaff High was successful. Teachers, parents and children were glad I was there. Some said it should have happened a long time ago. I was assigned to work with a math teacher in the morning and a science teacher in the afternoon. I could not have been in a better working and learning environment. Every one including teachers, children and parents treated me the same as they did the other teachers. It was wonderful.

I did have one very unpleasant experience in Flagstaff, but it was not at the school. It was in town. The science class was studying pulleys and some of them wanted to go down town to the Ford garage and see pulleys in action. The science teacher asked me to take a group of 12 to the garage in town. Everything at the garage went well. The staff answered questions from the students and invited them back anytime. On the way back to school we passed a café. The weather was warm that day. The walk from the school to town was about ten blocks. The students asked me if we could stop at the café for a coca cola or something cool to drink. Knowing how crazy the town was about not serving blacks I wanted to say no. But, then I thought, here I am an adult dressed in a suit with twelve teenagers, surely if I go in with them and don't order anything they won't say anything. We went in and sat around the tables.

The teens told the waiter what they wanted and offered to buy a drink for me. I thanked them and said I did not want anything. As the waiter was getting the children's drink the manager came out of the office in the back and told me he was sorry, but he could not serve me. I told him I did not want anything. I was a teacher doing my practice teaching at the high school and we were in town on a science project. On our way back to the school the students wanted to stop for a cold drink because it was a warm day. I told the manager I was not ordering anything, I was just waiting for the children.

"Well," he said, "You will just have to wait outside." There it was. What I was afraid of had just happened. I was so angry. I had a hard time controlling myself, but realized with the children there I could not act like a fool. I didn't say a word, I just got up and walked out. As I was going out he said, "I'm glad you're not giving me any trouble." If he only knew what I was thinking he would not have said that.

All of the students came out and said, "Mr. Camper, we are sorry. We didn't know. We don't want those drinks." I told them it was too bad that things like this happen and I was sorry that they had to experience it, but it was good for them to see and know how wrong that was.

I told them to stay in school, get an education and as adults pass laws that would not allow something like this to happen. Then I told them their drinks had been ordered and were on the table, go in pay and drink them. They said they did not want them. I instructed them that even if they did not drink them, they had to go in and pay for them. They went back in and paid for their drinks. Some drank theirs and some didn't.

I was sorry we had to go through something like this, but was glad I did not have any black students with me at the time. It was hard enough for the white students to accept. I was better able to accept the situation than my students for I had been subjected to this all my life. Maybe this is why the manager, even after being told I was a teacher supervising students, didn't stop to think or care how embarrassing it was for me for him to act as he did. He knew I was use to it. That made me think of something I heard on the playgrounds years ago when I was in elementary school.

[Two men were on death row, one black and the other white. The white man was crying and saying he didn't want to die. The black man asked him why he was carrying on so because he was going to die too, but he wasn't crying about it. The white man told the black man, "I know, but you folks are used to it." "Yes" said the black man, "but it hurts just as much."]

Yes, it hurts just as much. What a different world this would be if before we said or did harm to another person we could as the Navajo says, "Walk in my moccasins."

The children told the school staff what had happened. Many staff came to me and said they would not be going to that café any more and would ask their friends not to, also. I was surprised that many of the adults did not know this was going on in their town and it was not just that café, but every café in town except the one black café that served anyone. However, I saw no need to tell this to them. I also decided if I had a group like that out again and they wanted something cool to drink, we would stop at a soda pop machine.

Honorable Discharge

This is To Certify that

HAYWARD J. CAMPER, 39528118 Pt , Hq. Det., Sec. #2, Sta. Com.

Army of the United States

is hereby Honorably Discharged from the military service of the United States of America.

This certificate is awarded as a testimonial of Honest and Faithful Service to his country.

Given at Headquarters Camp Van Dorn, Mississippi

Date October 12, 1943

E. KENNEDY
MAJOR AGD
DIR PERS DIV

W. D., A. G. O. Form No. 55
January 22, 1943

PART III

CHAPTER 8

I graduated in May 1947 receiving my master of arts degree in education Although, I had been busy with my school work and taking care of my two boys, I also had been busy courting a nice young lady that had three children, was working and was as concerned about her children having a nice home and family as I was.

Her name was Isabell J. Dawson. She was born January 7, 1918 in Colfax, Louisiana to Joseph and Cora Lee Jones. She had two brothers, George and Marshall At the age of seven her parents divorced and her mother moved to Mc Nary, Arizona where she attended school through the eighth grade. She did very well in school, however, there was no high school there for black children. Isabell's teacher, her mother and her Uncle Ben got her books and encouraged her to read. They knew she would do well if she went to high school. She did a sort of home study for a while then got married to Andrew Dawson, a sawmill worker in Mc Nary and started a family.

When the marriage failed, she moved to Phoenix with her two daughters and a son to support. She did various jobs. Life was not easy with three children. In the meantime Isabell's mother remarried and moved to Flagstaff, Arizona. All of Isabell's family encouraged her to move to Flagstaff and live with her mother and her new husband, Johnny Todd. There Isabell could work and not have to worry about her three children, Gloria, Sybil Mae and Lawrence who would be home with her mother while she worked.

Isabell moved to Flagstaff and obtained a job at the Greyhound bus station as a dishwasher and later became a waitress. I met Isabell at the bus station. I went there often with my two sons to eat. She told me she admired the way I took care of my sons, Marvin and Maurice. I started visiting her at her mother's house and took an interest in her children too. Our children got along well with each other although her children were older then mine. We fell in love with each other. I asked her to marry me. She wasn't too sure about marriage after her experience with her first husband. But, I think we saw attributes in each other that we each desired from the opposite sex. AH! The courting stage was wonderful. Isabell loved the big baskets of yellow "glads" (gladiolas) I sent her. They became her favorite flower.

One day Isabell had a family conference with her children and asked them how they would feel about us getting married and putting the two families together. They were all for it. Her children let her know they wanted me for a father. Early one morning Isabell and I took a bus to Gallup, New Mexico to get married because there was a long waiting period to get married in Arizona. We wanted to get married right away. We were married May 23, 1947. Although we were one family in spirit and legally, her children did not have Camper as their last name. A year or so later we went to St. John, Arizona and went to court to take care of that.

I now had a loving wife, a family and a college degree!

I always thought Isabell was smarter than me even though I had a master's degree. She thought I was intellectual, but she could spell and pronounce words that I couldn't. I encouraged her to go to college and get her degree. She was excited about that because she always wanted to continue her education. So she took her GED, went to college and received her master's degree also. We would be able to work together in the field of education.

CHAPTER 9

Well, I was still working at the hotel until I could get a teaching job. My application was with the college placement office. I knew there would be nothing in Flagstaff. The elementary school for black students had their teachers and though I had had the opportunity to practice teach in their high school, they were not ready to give me a teaching job.

I had an aunt and sister in the Phoenix public school system where they had one black high school and two elementary schools so I thought I may get something there, but with summer business being so good at the hotel and a wife and five children I decided to stay where I had a job and wait on the college placement office to find me something.

It was near the end of summer when the placement office had a position for me at Mc Nary, Arizona. It was a principal-teaching job at Washington Elementary School. This was a small school for black students with a staff of three. I was to be the principal and teach the seventh and eighth grades. The salary wasn't that great. I was to get $3,000 a year and a company house to live in. The hotel manager thought I was crazy to take it. "You do much better than that here, don't you?" He asked. "Yes," I said "But now that I have gone to school, have my degree and teaching certificate, I want to use it." "Well, you may come back here and work any time, there will be a job waiting for you." He said.

It was good that I had been able to save while working and going to school in Flagstaff or I would not have had enough money to move to Mc Nary. My wife had also been working all that time. The fact that I was to be a teacher and a principal is what really attracted me. I was to be the boss, Boy OH Boy!

Mc Nary was a small sawmill town in northern Arizona on the Apache Indian Reservation. The land had been leased to Mr. Mc Nary for this sawmill. Since Mr. Mc Nary was from Louisiana he had his own ideas about how a town should be built and governed. The land at the bottom of a large incline was used to build his sawmill, living quarters, school, church, barber shop and restaurant for blacks and Hispanics. The land above was for all the other buildings and businesses of the town, and living quarters and schools for the white population. Also Hispanics were able to go to the high school with the whites, but their elementary school was in their living area, where they lived with the black population.

The first company house had so many bed bugs we had to move into another house the second day. The third day I was at my school working and seeing what I needed prior to school starting in about a month. The school superintendent, Mr. L. Pierce, a young man who was in his first year on the job, came to the school to visit and see what I needed to get started.

After our school business had been taken care of I asked him if the high school would be starting the same date as the elementary schools. He told me it was and wanted to know why I was asking. I told him I had a daughter in the ninth grade and my wife would be taking her to the high school for enrollment. "What! You have a daughter old enough for high school? I had no idea." He said. I told him I had a daughter for the ninth grade now and one in the eighth who will be ready for high school next year.

He told me he knew I had just completed college, but had no idea I had children high school age. He then informed me that he didn't have a high school there for black children. I told him in Flagstaff all the children went to the same high school no matter their race.

And, it's against the law not to have a high school for the black children. "How is this town getting away with this?" I asked.

"I know this isn't right, but this is my first year here. I will talk to Mr. Mc Nary and see what we can do," he said. This was a real mess. I was so happy about getting the job and here I was in a town that had no high school for black children. I could not accept that. I had a daughter in the ninth grade, now what was I going to do?

I talked to the two black teachers at the school. They thought I knew about the school situation. Some black parents sent their high school students to surrounding towns to stay with friends or relatives. Others would stay in town and get married. Boys, if they were old enough, would get a job at the sawmill. I started talking to the parents. Their men had good jobs at the sawmill and they didn't want to cause any trouble so they just let this happen, though they knew it wasn't right.

I wanted to leave, but we had spent most of our savings moving here. I had a job in Flagstaff waiting for me at the hotel where I could make more than twice what I was getting here, but then it was more than money. The black children in the town did not deserve this. I was an angry young man. Angry that I had jumped at and taken the first job that was offered to me; angry that many black parents saw jobs at the sawmill more important than their children's education; angry that all these years high school was available for other students, and none of the teaching staff at the black school had done anything to correct the situation.

Mc Nary school superintendent said he knew it wasn't right and he would see what he could do to correct the situation. I would wait and see what he could do. I knew this was so very wrong. Mr. Mc Nary and the Mc Nary school board would have to let the black children go to the high school with the other children. We were only talking about four students for the ninth grade. I told the parents of the other three students that the school superintendent was working to get the black students in Mc Nary High School.

Several weeks passed and I heard nothing. Finally the school superintendent came to my school to bring a large box of books. "Hayward," he said. "I have been working hard with the school board and Mr. Mc Nary to get your ninth graders in school with the other students. I am almost there, but I need a little more time. I have ninth grade texts here for you to get your four ninth graders started, then as soon as I get a few problems worked out, they will be transferred to Mc Nary High School with the other students."

I did not like this idea at all, but I didn't see where I had a choice. He seemed so sure of himself that it would only be a short time. I started the year teaching the 6th, 7th, 8th and 9th grades. School started the first week of September. We were in the last week of November and my ninth graders were still with me. Then the first week of December the school superintendent came to my school and said the problem had been taken care of. I was to continue teaching the ninth grade and for next fall they would move a portable building in and give me another teacher. I could have my own high school.

I was shocked and angry. I told the superintendent I wasn't about to be part of starting up such an inadequate system. He pointed out that in Phoenix the blacks had their own school. I told him the black school at Phoenix was very much below standard. They didn't have enough students to generate enough money to support a good education system and here we were only talking about four students.

He pointed out that once word got out that there was a black high school in Mc Nary children who had been sent out of town for high school would come back.

I asked him if he, the school board, or Mr. Mc Nary had checked this out with the office of education in Phoenix. He told me they had no need to because this is what the city of Phoenix was doing. I told him I wanted to check this out. He said he had no objections. He was sure they would agree with the Mc Nary School Board for the blacks to have their own high school.

I was really at a lost about what to do. I was angry and thought about quitting and going back to Flagstaff. Isabell thought that would be a cowardly thing to do, even though I thought it would be best for us. Our daughter would have a high school to go to, and working at the hotel, with salary and tips, I would more than double what I was making now. Also, Isabell could start college. I knew she would do well. She could spell and read better than me though I had a master's degree. I told her she had a better education than me – I just had the credit. However, it ended with us staying there to fight the situation.

top left - Blanche and me; top right - Isabel's Mother - Cora Lee Jones
bottom left - Blanche; bottom right - Blanche's first step

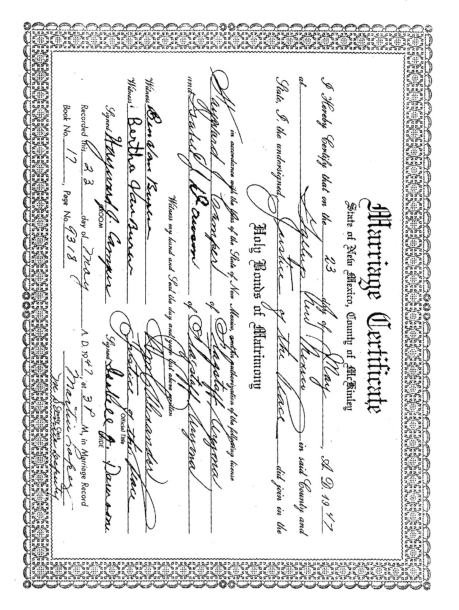

61

Hayward J. Camper

Arizona State College at Flagstaff

Greeting to all to whom these Letters shall come

The Board of Regents of the University and State Colleges
of Arizona by virtue of the authority bested in it by law and
on recommendation of the College Faculty does hereby confer on

Hayward James Camper

who has satisfactorily completed the Studies prescribed therefor
the Degree of

Master of Arts in Education

with all the Rights Privileges and Honors thereunto appertaining

In witness whereof the Seal of the College is hereto affixed

Done at Flagstaff Arizona this twenty-third day of May in the
year of our Lord one thousand nine hundred and forty-seven

PRESIDENT OF THE BOARD

SECRETARY OF THE BOARD

GOVERNOR OF ARIZONA

PRESIDENT OF THE COLLEGE

REGISTRAR OF THE COLLEGE

Arizona State College at Flagstaff

Greeting to all to whom these Letters shall come

The Board of Regents of the Universities and State College of Arizona by virtue of the authority vested in it by law and on recommendation of the College Faculty does hereby confer on

Isabell Jones Camper

who has satisfactorily completed the Studies prescribed therefor the Degree of

Master of Arts in Education

with all the Rights Privileges and Honors thereunto appertaining

In witness whereof the Seal of the College is hereto affixed Done at Flagstaff, Arizona this twenty-second day of May, in the year of our Lord one thousand nine hundred and fifty-nine

PRESIDENT OF THE BOARD

SECRETARY OF THE BOARD

GOVERNOR OF ARIZONA

PRESIDENT OF THE COLLEGE

REGISTRAR OF THE COLLEGE

ARIZONA STATE COLLEGE AT FLAGSTAFF · 1899 · GREAT SEAL OF THE STATE OF ARIZONA · 1912 · DITAT DEUS

Hayward J. Camper

Outstanding
Elementary Teachers of America

This is to certify that   ISABELL JOSEPHINE CAMPER

has been selected as an *Outstanding Elementary Teacher of America*
for 1972 in recognition of contributions to the advancement of
elementary education and service to community.

1972

V. Gilbert Beers
V. Gilbert Beers, Ph.D.
Director

Certificate of Leadership

Arizona Boys and Girls 4-H Club Work

Service Award

The Agricultural Extension Service of The University of Arizona and the United States

Department of Agriculture and _____ Navajo _____ County Cooperating

This Certifies that _____ Isabell J. Camper _____ of _____ White Cone "The Indians" _____ 4-H Club

has completed _____ One _____ year _____ of 4-H Club Leadership.

Date Awarded _September 18, 1961_

DIRECTOR, ARIZONA AGRICULTURAL EXTENSION SERVICE

COUNTY EXTENSION AGENT

STATE LEADER, 4-H CLUB WORK

65

UNITED STATES

DEPARTMENT OF THE INTERIOR

CS—Education

BUREAU OF INDIAN AFFAIRS
Navajo Agency
Window Rock, Arizona 86515

NOV 1 5 1965

Through: Subagency Superintendent, Fort Defiance Subagency
and School Superintendent

Mrs. Isabel Camper
Indian Wells Day School
Indian Wells, Arizona

Dear Mrs. Camper:

The Navajo Agency Branch of Education wishes to commend you on the fine
work you did as Demonstration Teacher at the Navajo Agency Orientation
Program, August 2 through August 14, 1965, at the Leupp Boarding School,
Leupp, Arizona.

You willingly accepted our request to be a demonstration teacher early
last spring. You started planning while school was still in session
and performed your regular duties as Principal-Teacher in the Indian
Wells Day School while doing all phases of this additional assignment
outside your regular tour of duty. You performed in a highly skilled
and professional manner before approximately 70 professionally trained
teachers daily for the duration of the orientation program.

Some of the duties that were necessary for you to perform were:

1. Arranging and making a classroom, approximately 80 miles
   from her duty station, functional and meaningfully attractive for pupils with whom you were working.

2. Preparing sufficient instructional material in
   advance to meet the anticipated wide range of ability
   of this primary grade class.

3. Developing rapport with your pupils in a new situation
   in order to demonstrate effectively teaching techniques
   which developed growth in areas of English as a Second
   Language, skill and content subjects.

66

4. Making comprehensive long-range plans in each area for the four weeks of work with the class, the last two of which were demonstrations for professionally trained teachers. These plans made use of the Basic Goals for Elementary Schools, the state course of study, resource materials and teaching aids suitable for primary grade children.

5. Breaking these plans into functional daily lesson plans in order to attain the long-range goals through a coordinated, sequential, and developmental program.

6. Using community resources, visual aids and field trips to develop concepts necessary for the attainment of immediate objectives and overall goals.

You made a comprehensive study of each child to determine his reading achievement before grouping your pupils. You selected and prepared appropriate materials from the standpoint of interest and instructional value for each child. The work you presented was varied in order to give each individual an opportunity to work at his own level of achievement and to participate constructively in group work.

You were alert and skillful in changing procedures and techniques when those being used failed in their desired effectiveness or when interest faded.

On analysis of your work, the Navajo Agency Branch of Education is pleased to present you with a Certificate of Appreciation, which we hope you will accept with a knowledge that your demonstration class was one of the keystones of the 1965 Navajo Agency Orientation Program.

Sincerely yours,

Acting Assistant General Superintendent
(Community Services)

**UNITED STATES
DEPARTMENT OF THE INTERIOR**
BUREAU OF INDIAN AFFAIRS
Navajo Agency
Window Rock, Arizona 86515

CS:Education

August 16, 1965

Mrs. Isabel Camper
Indian Wells Day School
Indian Wells, Arizona

Dear Mrs. Camper:

As demonstration teacher at the 1965 Navajo Agency Orientation Program
held at Leupp Boarding School on August 2 to August 13, you played a vital
role in preparing the new teachers for their first year of teaching on the
Navajo Reservation. For your excellent contribution, we express the
appreciation of the Navajo Agency Branch of Education and the participants.

Thank you for the many hours of devoted service you gave toward the improvement of education for Navajo children.

Sincerely,

Assistant General Superintendent
(Community Services)

IN REPLY REFER TO:

UNITED STATES
DEPARTMENT OF THE INTERIOR
BUREAU OF INDIAN AFFAIRS
Navajo Agency
Fort Defiance Subagency
Fort Defiance, Arizona

Education

January 19, 1965

Memorandum

To: Mrs. Isabell Camper, Principal-Teacher
        Indian Wells Day School

From: Subagency School Superintendent

Subject: Appreciation for Services

Isabell, you are one very fine teacher and we have appreciated all you have done since you have been in the Fort Defiance Subagency.

I want you to know that my best wishes go with you and your fine husband in your future service.

Carson V. Ryan
Subagency School Superintendent

UNITED STATES
DEPARTMENT OF THE INTERIOR
BUREAU OF INDIAN AFFAIRS
NAVAJO AGENCY
WINDOW ROCK, ARIZONA 86515

CS—Education

September 17, 1964

Mrs. Isabel Camper
Principal - Teacher
Indian Wells Day School
Indian Wells, Arizona

Dear Mrs. Camper:

We express our sincere appreciation to you for the excellent contribution you made to the 1964 Navajo Agency Orientation Program as a discussion leader of the Oral English Program for Navajo children. Through your efforts, we believe the new teachers have received the professional assistance so necessary in their first year of teaching on the Navajo.

On behalf of the Agency Branch of Education we thank you for this.

Sincerely yours,

Assistant General Superintendent
(Community Services)

Certificate of Leadership

Arizona Boys and Girls 4-H Club Work

Service Award

The Agricultural Extension Service of The University of Arizona and the United States

Department of Agriculture and _____ Navajo _____ County Cooperating

This Certifies that _Isabell J. Camper_ _____ of _White Cone "The Indians"_ 4-H Club

has completed _____ One _____ year_ of 4-H Club Leadership.

Date Awarded _September 18, 1961_

George E. Hull

DIRECTOR, ARIZONA AGRICULTURAL EXTENSION SERVICE

Graham P. Wright

STATE LEADER, 4-H CLUB WORK

Lou B. Wark

COUNTY EXTENSION AGENT

71

Hayward J. Camper

AMERICAN CORRECTIONAL ASSOCIATION

Commission On Accreditation For Corrections
and the
American Correctional Association

awards

ACCREDITATION

to

New Mexico Corrections Department
Youth Diagnostic and Development Center
Albuquerque, New Mexico

in recognition of the attainment of excellence in the operation of

Juvenile Training School

presented this 4th day of August 1987

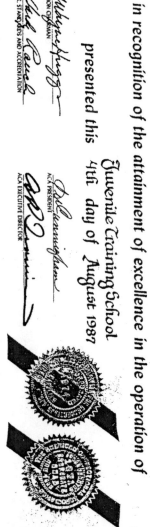

COMMISSION CHAIRMAN

DIRECTOR, STANDARDS AND ACCREDITATION

ACA PRESIDENT

ACA EXECUTIVE DIRECTOR

STATE OF NEW MEXICO
CORRECTIONS DEPARTMENT

TONEY ANAYA, *Governor*
MICHAEL FRANCKE, *Secretary*

113 Washington Avenue
Santa Fe, New Mexico 87501
(505) 827-8647

December 15, 1983

Mr. Hayward J. Camper
Youth Diagnostic and Development Center
P. O. Box 6038 Station B
Albuquerque, New Mexico 87107

Dear Mr. Camper:

The Juvenile Facilities and Programs Division has made significant progress in the last year toward improving the services
offered Juveniles under our care.

I would personally like to thank you for your efforts on behalf
of Juveniles in need of help and wish you a Merry Christmas and a
New Year more exciting and profitable than this year.

Sincerely,

LLOYD MIXDORF, Director
Juvenile Facilities Division

LM:bt

The Gallup NM Independent—Tuesday, September 26, 1972—Page 3

Greasewood Teachers Receive Awards

Three Greasewood Boarding School teachers have been selected as Outstanding Elementary teachers of America for 1972. They are Helen Kanyid, Isabell Camper, and Dan Hundley.

Miss Kanyid is in charge of Greasewood's Resource Center, where she and her aid, Marjorie Jimmie, work with children in beginners through fourth grade who have various types of learning disabilities. She helped two years ago to write the proposal for the Resource Center project. The project was accepted and is now funded under title I of Public Law 89-10.

Mrs. Camper has worked for three years in the CITE program at Greasewood. CITE (Consultants in Total Education) is a special program for the education of young Navajo children in which all lessons are scripted and must be presented exactly as directed. It requires a great deal of "homework" on the part of the teacher. Mrs. Camper taught beginners and first grade at Greasewood for several years before going into the CITE program. She is now teaching a first grade CITE class.

Dan Hundley teaches upper elementary science. Last year, in addition to teaching six classes daily, he worked with Boy Scouts, initiated a community ecology program, and taught an adult first aid class for the Red Cross.

The three teachers were nominated earlier this year by teacher supervisor Helen Zongolowicz and principal Hayward Camper.

They were selected for this

OUTSTANDING ELEMENTARY Teachers of America for 1972—Dan Hundley, Helen Kanyid and Isabell Camper are teachers at Greasewood Boarding School. The high honor distinguishes men and women who have shown their leadership and outstanding service in the field of elementary education.

national honor on the basis of their professional and civic achievements.

Outstanding Elementary Teachers of America is an annual program honoring the men and women who have distinguished themselves by their service and leadership in the field of elementary education. Each year, the biographies of those honored are featured in the awards volume "Outstanding Elementary Teachers of America."

In announcing the award winners to the school principal, Dr. V. Gilbert Beers, director of the Outstanding Elementary Teachers of America program cited them for their exceptional service.

"The men and women chosen for this high honor," Dr. Beers said, "have explored new paths, developed new insights, and effectively communicated their knowledge to their students and colleagues. They are the exceptional teachers."

Guidelines for selection include a teacher's talents in the classroom, civic service and professional recognition.

Dr. Beers, in addition to directing the national education awards program, is a noted teacher, writer and editor of educational publications. He holds a Ph.D. from Northwestern University and additional degrees from Wheaton College and Northern Baptist Theological Seminary.

74

CHAIRMAN RAYMOND NAKAI is speaking with student, George Franc; as they chat on the type of food and the school activities of the newl dedicated Greasewood Boarding School which has been in operati since September 1, 1964. The above picture was taken in the dini hall of the new school. (Staff Photo)

Window Rock, Arizona · November 26, 1964

Greasewood Boardin₅ School Dedication

Approximately 500 persons viewed the Greasewood Boarding School located 22 miles southwest of Ganado, Arizona where the dedication was held on Friday, Nov. 20 for the 690 pupils of which the school now totals. There are four 160-pupil dormitories; an academic building with 23 classrooms; library; multi-purpose room; preview room; school office; dining room and kitchen.

There are also 52 new two and three-bedroom houses, 20 new efficiency apartments, a maintainance shop and a fire station.

The new Greasewood Boarding School has been in operation since September. 1, 1964 having a full enrollment with about 50 day students who either live close enough to walk in 'or they are brought in on the school bus.

Joe Yazzie, Navajo medicineman, blessed the building in the gymnasium where the dedication was held. The invocation was given by Father Simon; welcoming address by Kathleen Stewart, 8th grade student at Greasewood Boarding School. The main speaker of the dedication was Chairman of the Navajo Tribal Council, Raymond Nakai who said, "This is one more step toward the progress of getting in line of my aim; seat every Navajo child eligib; to attend a government school ⁞ the Reservation. The Bureau ; constructing new facilities to reac that goal in the not too far dis tant future."

Anna Miles representing th Branch of Education gave the clos ing remarks and said, "The tw languages of Navajo and Englis are necessary today in becomin an outstanding student as well a a successful businessman for Navajo student."

Benediction was given by Ec ward Tsosie in Navajo.

Guests in attendance includec

(Continued on Page ⁞

KATHLEEN STEWART, 8th gra student at the new Greasewo Boarding School gave the welcoming address at the school dedication on Friday, November 20. Sh₅ is one of the students who has aı outstanding achievement in civic affairs.

75

Hayward J. Camper

UNITED STATES DEPARTMENT OF THE INTERIOR

Bureau of Indian Affairs

CERTIFICATE
of
SUPERIOR PERFORMANCE

granted to

HAYWARD J. CAMPER

In recognition of service performed in a manner
exceeding the requirements of ___his___ position.

Granted this ___13th___ day of ___August___, 19_65_

SUPERINTENDENT

76

UNITED STATES DEPARTMENT OF THE INTERIOR PERFORMANCE RATING REPORT	Period covered *(from, to)* April 1, 1962 to March 31, 1963.
Employee's name *(first, initial, last)* **Isabell J. Camper**	Position, title, grade **Teacher (Elem) E40.4529 GS-07**
Organization and headquarters Greasewood Boarding School - Branchoof Education - Fort Defiance Subagency	

INSTRUCTIONS.—Prepare in duplicate. Consult detailed instructions in the Performance Rating Instructions to Rating and Reviewing Officials. Rate elements 1 to 4. Rate supervisors on element 5 as well. Additional elements may be added in item 6 and on the reverse side if important requirements of the job are not adequately covered in elements 1 to 5. Any rating element marked "Unsatisfactory" must be supplemented with an explanatory statement.

	RATING ELEMENTS		INDICATE BY "X"			
			Unsatis-factory	Satis-factory	Excel-lent	Out-standing
1. Volume of work	Degree to which quantity of work turned out meets requirements.	Consider: Amount of work produced; rate of progress on assignments.				X
2. Quality of work	Degree to which quality of the work meets requirements.	Consider: Accuracy, precision, completeness, and acceptability of work.			X	
3. Work habits	Degree to which employee facilitates work of others.	Consider: Organization of work; observance of rules and procedures; observance of safety rules; cooperation and tact; conduct on the job; dependability.				X
4. Work attitude	Degree to which employee applies himself to job.	Consider: Enthusiasm for the work; acceptance of supervision; adaptability to changing conditions; willingness to accept responsibility.				X
5. Supervisory ability	Degree to which supervisor obtains results from those under his supervision.	Consider: Effectiveness in directing and reviewing the work of others, establishing standards of performance, training subordinates, and delegating authority.				
Other (specify) 6.						

SUMMARY RATING

Date	Rating official *(signature and title)*					
5-1-63	*Mary Anita Rice - Edu. Spec, Elem*					X
Date 5-3-63	Reviewing official *(signature and title)* *[signature]* Agency School Superintendent					X
Date	For unsatisfactory or outstanding ratings only: Designated official or committee chairman *(signature and title)*					

DEFINITIONS OF SUMMARY RATINGS

Outstanding: Performance of which all aspects not only exceed normal requirements but are outstanding and deserve special commendation.

Excellent: Performance which fully meets all requirements and which exceeds such requirements in the majority of the principal duties of the position.

Satisfactory: Performance which meets requirements in the principal duties of the position.

Unsatisfactory: Performance which fails to meet requirements of the position.

U.S. GOVERNMENT PRINTING OFFICE: 1960 O - 575544   GPO #24835

Hayward J. Camper

IN REPLY REFER TO:

UNITED STATES
DEPARTMENT OF THE INTERIOR
BUREAU OF INDIAN AFFAIRS
Navajo Area Office
Window Rock, Navajo Nation (Arizona) 86515

Education

AUG 29 1969

Memorandum

To: School Superintendent, Fort Defiance Agency
        Attention: Mrs. Isabelle Camper

Through: Principal, Greasewood Boarding School

From: Assistant Area Director (Education)

Subject: Letter of Appreciation

The Navajo Area Division of Education wishes to express its sincere appreciation for your services to the BIA-NAEYC and the Title III Bilingual-Bicultural Kindergarten Workshops. The morning coffee breaks and the afternoon teas were well attended by participants and staff members.

The various displays of art work and hobbies exhibited by the Greasewood Boarding School staff members were enjoyed by all.

Please convey the appreciation of the Navajo Area to all who assisted you.

Abraham I. Tucker

ACTING Assistant Area Director (Education)

CHAPTER 10

Isabell and I wrote a letter to the state superintendent of schools in Phoenix, Arizona about the school situation in Mc Nary and asked for a request from his office that the black children be allowed to go to Mc Nary High School with the other boys and girls. We then got as many signatures from parents as we could to show support for our cause. Many did not want to sign for fear of a husband or son losing their job at the sawmill. We understood this and did not pressure anyone. Just before the Christmas holidays we mailed the letter.

Who can I blame for this situation? Really, I could blame no one. As a child in Prescott I thought it was raining in the yard next door and not in our yard because the family was white. In church we san a song, "What can wash away my sins, nothing but the blood of Jesus. What can make me white as snow, nothing but the blood of Jesus." All the people in charge of things were white. Yes, I would have liked to have been white. No, I can't blame the little white boys for throwing rocks at me, laughing and saying, "That's it, nigger, dance the jig."

Maybe, the adults should know better, but when I come up in an environment like this, what are you to think? It took a long while for me to feel that I could do as much as the next fellow, no matter what race. However, to be a success in life you need the proper environment as well as believing in yourself. White teachers needed to expect the same from black students as they did from their white children. Schools cannot expect to do it all. Parents have their role. Schools through parent teacher conferences should be able to bring all the children into an inclusive environment.

The year is 1947. No way was I going to be part of a school system that does not give black children the same quality of education as the other children have.

The second or third week of March the state superintendent of schools came to my school with Mc Nary's school superintendent. We had a long meeting. It ended with the state superintendent telling Mc Nary's superintendent that the school could continue for the rest of year as was, but in September he wanted and expected Mc Nary High School to be open for black students and if necessary he would send law officers from Phoenix to Mc Nary to see that it was done. He also told the superintendent he expected to hear from me if it wasn't done, and for him not to think of getting with the Mc Nary school board and Mr. Mc Nary to get rid of me.

The next day Mc Nary's superintendent, Mr. Pierce was back at my school. He said Mr. Mc Nary was very angry and said the state superintendent should have met with him. He also told Mr. Pierce that he should fire both of us. I didn't know what to expect. I really wanted to leave at the end of the school year, but I also wanted to stay until the blacks were going to high school with the other children. My wife and I decided to stay.

The summer of 1949 I went back to Flagstaff and worked at the hotel. The manager wanted me to stay, but I told him I had to go back.

Three weeks before the fall term I was back in Mc Nary getting ready for school to start. The black community was feeling good that their high school children would be going to school with the other children. However, none of them who had children in other towns were going to bring them home. I did have my ninth graders ready to go there for the 10th grade and three eight graders for the ninth grade.

Two weeks before school was to start I was working at the school when Mr. Pierce came in acting very nervous and asked me how the black community felt. I told him they were happy that their children would be going to school with the other children. Then he said, "The school board will have a high school for the black children, but it is not quite ready. They have a building on order, but it has not arrived yet. Once it gets here they will place it on the grounds with the other buildings and hire a teacher.

I could not believe what I was hearing. How stupid could I get? Though I started the 1949 school year teaching the seventh through tenth grades, I made a trip to Phoenix and told the superintendent what was going on. He was shocked and upset. He told me my high school children would be going to the Mc Nary high school. I do not know what action he took, but several days later the Mc Nary school superintendent told me there had been a change in plans and to bring my ninth and tenth graders to the Mc Nary High School for enrollment.

Before the school year was over, I pulled another stunt that upset them. They had some activity at the movie theater for all the school children. I took my children and went with them to the balcony. Blacks were always required to sit in the balcony when they went to the movie. One of my students asked me why we couldn't sit down stairs with the other schools. I couldn't say there wasn't enough room because there were plenty of empty seats after the other schools were seated. I didn't want to cause a problem, but we could hear and have a better view of the program, if we sat downstairs. The few black high school children were sitting with their class, so I told my two teachers we would go down stairs and sit. As soon as we sat down the manager came over and told me to take my students back upstairs. Then he said the school superintendent said they were to sit in the balcony. They already had some high school niggers sitting with their class down stairs and he did not intend to have any more.

I started to take my children back to the school, I was so stirred with anger. The school superintendent's office was only a few doors from the theater, so I told the manager I would check with

81

the superintendent. I walked to the superintendent's office. He saw I was upset. I asked him why my students had to sit in the balcony where they couldn't hear or see the program well. He said, "Hayward, I don't care whey they sit." I returned to the theater and told the manager. He was very angry and hurried back to his office slamming the door.

The next morning the school superintendent was at my school before I got there. "Hayward," he said, "you just don't know when to quit. Your children are going to high school with the other children and sitting in the theater with their class. That alone was an accomplishment, but, no, you are not satisfied. You knew the policy of blacks going to the balcony to sit and yet you pushed it to have your children not sit in the balcony. You can't come to this town and expect them to change all their ways of doing things to suit you. School will be out in another month. Mr. Mc Nary has requested you be out of your house in a week because the new school principal and his family will be coming in early." "My family and I are leaving the day after school is out," I said. He left without another word.

CHAPTER 11

At the end of May 1949 my family and I moved back to Flagstaff. I started working at the Monte Vista Hotel again. I decided to do that until I got another teaching position. The placement office at the college had my application and they were looking for a job for me. I was sure I would have something soon with my qualifications. I had my master's degree and two years' experience as a principal/teacher. Since the demand for black teachers was only great in the Phoenix area where they had two black elementary schools and one high school, I was hoping for a position there.

I had an aunt and sister already working in that area. I heard some disturbing news. My sister heard some of the teachers talking and saying, "You remember reading in the paper about that fellow that was giving all that trouble in Mc Nary? Well, he wants to come here to work. We don't need him here." I knew the Phoenix paper had some articles about the school problem in Mc Nary, but I never bothered to collect the articles. Now I wish I had. I have tried since to get copies, but with no luck.

After hearing the news from my sister that I was considered a trouble maker and a communist, I thought I may as well forget about another teaching job.

One of my duties working at the hotel was to go to the post office down the street to take the outgoing mail and pick up the hotel mail. I noticed on their bulletin board that teachers were needed on the

Navajo reservation. This teaching position was at Toadlena, New Mexico. The pay wasn't much, a GS-3 position at $2,650 a year. This was less than the $3,000 a year I was making at Mc Nary, but it was a teaching position and that is what I wanted and went to school for.

Was this an impossible dream? I have a wife and five children, the older two in high school and a wife that wanted to go to college. We didn't stop to think about if. If we had we may have decided this was an impossible mission. I knew Isabell would do well in college. She took the GED test, passed with high marks and was ready for college. We finally rented a cottage on campus and she enrolled. She was majoring in education with a minor in home economics.

I applied for the teaching position on the Navajo reservation and was selected to teach the sixth grade at Toadlena Boarding School in Toadlena, New Mexico. Though I had lived out west most of my life I had never before given any thought about the reservation so I didn't really know where I was going or what I was getting myself into. I took a bus to Gallup, New Mexico and someone from the school met me in Gallup and took me to the school. The trip to Gallup seemed like forever, but it was nothing like the ride to Toadlena. I thought I must be crazy. I didn't own a car. I didn't even know how to drive. How was I going to see my family? When would I see them again? We turned off of Highway 666 at Newcomb on a dirt road to Toadlena. Now I knew I had made a mistake, but it was too late to back out. I would give it a try.

I was given a room in the clubhouse with a large kitchen for cooking. I arranged for my pay check to go to Isabell to take care of family needs, then she could send me what she could. I don't know how she did it, but with the help of the two older children they managed to budget and send money to me. They were really living on the edge doing mission impossible. She could write an interesting story.

My main diet was oatmeal for breakfast, no lunch and pinto beans for dinner. On weekends, since I had no car and no where to go, I helped staff with the children and ate my noon meal with them. Now and then I rode with one of the other teachers to Gallup to buy food. The trading post was too expensive. The trader said he gave so much credit and waited so long for his money that he had to have high prices. He said he was giving me a break because I paid cash. I couldn't see the break he was giving me.

After my experience in Mc Nary, I did not know what to expect on the reservation. There were nine teachers at Toadlena and three were black. The Navajos on the reservation were friendly. They did ask me why black teachers were hired to teach their children, but not to teach white children. I did not have the answer to that question.

The towns bordering the reservation had no black teachers unless they had a black school. I could not stay overnight in any of their hotels. Going to Gallup on weekends I had to get back to Toadlena to sleep or rent a room from some black family in Gallup. I was not welcome in eating places. I did observe another crazy custom. Navajo teachers had trouble getting a job because it was felt that they would use too much Navajo in the classroom and we were to encourage students to talk English all the time. I have heard that children were punished for speaking Navajo

I wanted none of that. Now there is a big turnaround. Today children are encouraged to use Navajo and English and there is Navajo preference for all jobs in the schools. Also, public schools have no all-black schools now. A limited number of black teachers are teaching in the schools and a few have black principals. Hotels and restaurants also serve blacks.

Isabell completed college and was hired to teach at Toadlena. Our girls stayed in Flagstaff for school. Our older son went to a boarding school on the reservation and the two younger boys to a public school at Toadlena. Now that both my wife and I were working we were able to buy a car. Our older children gave us driving lessons. In retrospect, I don't know how we ever managed without a car.

The school superintendent, Miss Dorothy Main had several schools under her supervision: Newcomb Day School, Tohatchi Boarding School, Naschitti Boarding School, Twin Lakes Boarding School and Toadlena Boarding School. Toadlena was the largest of the schools and that's where she had her office. She appreciated my help on weekends, going out into the community checking on children who had gone home and not returned to school, and helping with the off-reservation enrollment of children from Inter Mountain, Phoenix and Albuquerque Indian School where buses would come to Toadlena to pick up and deliver children.

Miss Main also recognized my wife as an outstanding teacher. When the two- teacher day school at Newcomb became vacant she offered the positions to us. This would give me the title of principal teacher with a higher grade and an increase in pay. Also our children could be home with us except our oldest daughter who was in nursing school in Albuquerque. A school bus ran up and down Highway 666 taking high school children to Kirtland for high school and grade school children to Shiprock for school.

Newcomb was about 25 miles from Toadlena on Highway 666. The school had beginners through third grades. Isabell had beginners and first grade and I had the second and third grades. Mr. and Mrs. Yazzie worked for us, he as the bus driver and his wife as the cook. We gave the children a meal at noon. And, we had nice large government houses to live in. I went with the bus driver enough times that I could drive the bus if he was not able to. I also got to know the parents of the children. The community was very friendly and parents felt free to visit the school at any time.

My driving the bus brought me closer to the community and though many of them went to the trader at the Trading Post with personal problems, some would come to me. I had gotten to know the parents at Toadlena, but there was a closeness at Newcomb I did not have at Toadlena. I guess one of the best things was not having any run-a-ways. Having run-a-ways in boarding school was one of our biggest problems. We would encourage parents to get their children on weekends and holidays. If it was a holiday like Christmas and the parent was not able to come, we would take the child home and go back after the vacation to bring the child back to school. Parents were encouraged to visit the school and children were encouraged to write their parents. If there was sickness in the family or for any reason a child was worried about a family member we would see to it that that child got home for a visit. Though we did everything we could to keep a student from running away, a few did run away.

When there was a run-a-way, a staff person went at once to look for the child and notify the parents. We also would report the run-a-way to the Navajo Police and Area Education Office. Staff would search until the child was found.

For some reason it seemed that when the weather was worse, someone would take off. Sometimes we would follow snow tracks to a Hogan and the people living there would hide the child and tell us they had not seen him or her. We would leave and continue looking and they would get the child to the parent. They did not want to give the child to school staff since the child ran away from school. Most of the run-a-ways were older children, but sometimes they would take a younger brother or sister with them.

The beginners were six years and this was their first time away from home. They had a hard time getting used to the new environment. I felt so sorry for them. They would cry and staff would do all they could to help, but it was usually several months before they became a little used to things.

If the roads had been kept in better condition, there could have been more day schools and fewer boarding schools. However, there were few paved roads. Hogans were spread far from each other, and in wet weather the roads were almost impassable.

CHAPTER 12

We had several good years at Newcomb before the state decided to build a large public school and run buses up and down Highway 666 as well as off the highway on the roads we traveled to pick up and deliver children. This of course meant the Bureau of Indian Affairs (BIA) school would be closing. The parents in the area wanted my wife and me to stay and seeing the nice new buildings going up and knowing so many of the families in the area I wanted to stay.

I thought about being asked at Toadlena why blacks were hired to teach the Navajo children but not the white children. I never thought much about it until now. I realized the public schools did not hire blacks to teach in any school except black schools. However, I decided to give it a try. I sent paperwork to Santa Fe, New Mexico and received teaching and administrative certificates for New Mexico. I received written requests from the chapter officers in the area for us to work at the new school.

I had the qualification for any of three positions: principal, teacher-supervisor and teacher. In my visit with the school superintendent at Kirtland I carried this information as well as a letter from the chapter officers in the area. The school superintendent said he had most of the positions filled, but would keep my wife and me in mind and let us know if we were to be hired. This didn't sound promising to me, but I had a little hope that the school being so far from town, he would have trouble filling his positions and hire us.

The new facilities at Newcomb were looking better every day. Not just the school buildings, but also the living quarters for employees. Then there was the fact that our own boys in grade school could stay home for school and our daughter in high school could continue at Kirtland. We had both applied for educational leave, which had been approved, but if we did not stay with the government we would have to pay that salary back. We told our supervisor we expected to stay and he said he would contact us at summer school when he had a location for us.

We were in summer school at flagstaff for about three weeks when the BIA supervisor said he had a position for us at White Cone Trailer School, in Indian Wells, Arizona. We had never heard of Indian Wells and asked other BIA employees in summer school about it and found several who knew about the school and where it was. It was fifty some miles north of Holbrook, Arizona. We picked up a road map from the service station and that weekend drove to White Cone.

The road off the main highway to White Cone was a rough dirt road. There were some portable buildings for classrooms, kitchen, and dining room, trailers for living quarters, and also trailers with showers and rest rooms for the students. There was a hut with a small power plant for electricity and to pump water. There were no telephones, but the Quonset hut I was to use for a classroom had a two-way radio to contact the area office and the Navajo police.

Keams Canyon, on the Hopi reservation about 25 miles from White Cone, had a boarding school. It was the nearest place for school for our boys. Our daughter would have to stay with someone in Flagstaff for high school. She was about ready for college and we had Flagstaff in mind.

This wasn't a very promising outlook. The trailer was one bedroom and much too small for my family. There was hardly enough room to move around. No way was I going to accept a position here I thought. Then some of my BIA friends told me if I didn't accept it, since they were closing my school at Newcomb, I would be given one more offer and if I didn't take that I would be out of a job.

89

Another offer could be farther out on the Navajo reservation not near any town and my hope of getting a position in Arizona Public School system wasn't bright since Mc Nary.

I then tried to think of positive things about the location. I was not too far from a main highway. I was near Holbrook, Winslow and Flagstaff. Also I was not far from Gallup. The bureau was going to move another trailer in for my family. Being a principal-teacher I would keep my GS rating and salary, which would be less, if I were only in a teacher position. The government was building a number of large schools on the reservation. The work and experience here may prepare me for a promotion.

The move to White Cone turned out to be one of my best decisions except for the fact I had to have all my children away for school. White Cone topped any community I had lived in. The people at no time considered me an outsider. My wife and I were invited to and welcomed to all of their community activities.

Living like this, miles away from town with no paved roads in the area, depending on a small power plant for water and electricity and no health care services near, one would say was a disadvantage, but the advantages were greater. The community depended on each other. We were like a big family working and helping one another. It was really like being on duty twenty-four hours a day, seven days a week. Isabell also started a 4-H club for the children and had the parents involved. We all just had a lot of fun.

As our program increased, we had added three bus runs, another trailer brought in and a teacher hired for an adult education program. Our education program for the children was beginners through fourth grade. We gave the children a light breakfast and a meal at noon. There were other trailer schools on the reservation, Indian Wells and Low Mountain that I would hear each morning on the radio in my classroom making their reports to the agency office.

We were at White Cone for a year and the road from Holbrook was being paved. Three large houses were built for the teaching staff, another Quonset was brought in for a classroom and another teacher hired. Isabell's classroom was a real showplace. She had many interest centers for the children. The agency supervisor, Mr. Carson Ryan would bring beginning teachers to her room to observe. She was also selected as one of the demonstration teachers in the summer for the bureau's orientation programs.

After the road to Holbrook was paved, Holbrook had a school bus running up and down the road to take children to Holbrook for school. My sons were able to be home which was nice. They did have a long ride to school every day. The younger son was in sports. He had football practice after school so I had to drive into Holbrook sometimes to get him.

Things at White Cone were going so well the government decided to build a large boarding school there for grades beginners through eighth grades. The community was overjoyed. Their older children would not have to leave the area for school and also there would be employment for many of the local people. Plans were drawn and everyone was smiling and talking about the new school. Then with completed plans and the community thinking a new school was on the way, it was decided there was not enough water in the area to support a large school. They would have to build it at Greasewood where they had plenty of water. This was a real disappointment for everyone. Now more than 50 years later, they are building there. Perhaps they found a way to get more water.

The fall of 1961 they decided to close the school at White Cone and I was transferred to Greasewood Boarding School as principal. Greasewood was a small boarding school about 15 miles south of White cone and 25 miles south of Ganado, Arizona. There were two dormitories and a bus run to pick up children in the area. The school had grades beginners through eight. Most of the White Cone students would be in the dormitory.

The move to Greasewood was a promotion for me from principal-teacher, GS-9 to principal, GS-11. Our boys would ride a bus to Ganado for school. However, there was one problem for us. Since the school was a small boarding school, the agency educational supervisor did not supervise the teachers. This was my responsibility and the policy was that I could not supervise my wife, so she was offered a position as principal-teacher at Indian Wells Trailer School, which she accepted. I never have been able to understand how she, one of the best teachers in the Bureau, demonstration teacher at work shops and orientation, ran circles around me as a teacher in the classroom, could not be allowed to teach at Greasewood and every now and then the agency supervisor or bureau school superintendent could drop in and see how things were going.

Indian Wells Trailer School was a one-teacher school with beginners and first grades, a bus driver and a cook. All the buildings were trailers. The children had a light breakfast in the morning and a meal at noon. The school was between White Cone and Holbrook. Most weekends Isabell was home at Greasewood unless the weather was bad. She did get an increase in grade from teacher GS-7 to principal-teacher GS-9. As always, she put all her energy into her work and the school became one of the show places for supervisors to take new teachers.

Several months before going to Indian Wells, Isabell was one of the substitute teachers for the area, so the position at Indian Wells was a blessing since she didn't have to be on the road driving from one school to another. The Greasewood community was not as friendly as the White Cone community. They weren't negative towards me, but didn't welcome me with open arms as the White Cone community had. To tell the truth the White Cone community had just spoiled me. I did, however, get an uplift in spirit when White Cone parents came to the school to see about their children. They always would stop at the office for a short visit with me.

As the Greasewood parents got to know me they became more friendly. I encouraged parents to visit the school any time and to take their children home on weekends. At Christmas we had a large community dinner. Parents with no transportation to take their children home for the holidays, we took them and picked them up after the Christmas break.

One would think the way blacks had been treated and were discriminated against, they would not practice the same on another person because of race. I had a white teacher married to a black man who was my guidance counselor. Three of my black teachers tried to make her life a living hell. They would not speak to her even when she spoke to them. At staff meetings they would try to cut her off when she tried to speak. I immediately had a meeting with them and told them their foolishness would have to stop. I would not allow it. I would send an unsatisfactory rating to personnel with a recommendation that they be terminated.

After my meeting with them, they wrote a letter to my supervisor, Mr. Ryan, the agency school superintendent asking that he visit the school as soon as possible. There was conflict between teachers, favoritism shown, low moral, conduct of some workers below standard, a constant upheaval to humiliate the older teachers, gossiping and misrepresentation of those teachers in the school.

I got a carbon copy of their letter. They also sent a copy to the personnel officer. I couldn't believe it. I had not done a write-up on them. I had only met and told them to change their behavior or I would do a write-up. They decided to move forward and "do one" on me.

Hayward J. Camper

Greasewood Brdg. School
Ganado, Arizona

December 14, 1961

Mr. Carson V. Ryan
Subagency School Superintendent
Fort Defiance Subagency
Fort Defiance, Arizona

Through:
  Mr. Camper
  Mr. Ryan
  Mr. Zweifel
  Personnel

Attention: Greasewood Boarding School

The undersigned would appreicate very much for you to come to Greasewood Boarding School at your earliest convenience.

The administration of the school seemly is not one of creditable standards. There are many things that are happening which are causing conflicts between teachers. There is definite favoritism shown certain persons. The morale of some of the personnel is very low. The moral conduct of some of the other workers is below standards.

There are constance upheavals to humiliate the older teachers in the school by untruthful gossiping and misrepresentations of these teachers in the school.

There are many things happening which cannot be stated in a letter. These things that cannot be mentioned are not of professional standards.

We have been called into question about such things as small children going into the fourth grade classroom; beginners running in the hall, record players, and the reorganization of 4-H clubs.

Please see to it that none of these things go into our folders.

c.c. Mr. Camper
    Mr. Ryan
    Mr. Zweifel
    Personnel

Yours truly,

Distressed teachers:

Mrs. Leora H. Lovelady
Mrs. Caroline J. Coleman
Neal L. Coleman

Navajo Agency
Fort Defiance Subagency
Fort Defiance, Arizona

January 23, 1962

Administratively Restricted

Mrs. Caroline J. Coleman
Greasewood Boarding School
Ganado, Arizona

Dear Mrs. Coleman:

On Wednesday, December 20, 1961, Mr. Bob Tillman, Acting Subagency Administrative Officer, and I visited Greasewood School and had a conference with you and Mr. Camper. This letter is to verify that conference for your personnel file and the record.

In the above cited conference it was pointed out to you that the contents of the letter dated December 14, 1961, and the copies that were sent constituted a malicious charge against Mr. Camper and if left unchallenged would certainly not enhance his future in the education field. In the same letter , you requested that no mention of such charges should go into your personnel folder.

You were informed that Mr. Camper had the right to refute such charges and that both the letter of the 14th and your written retraction of the letter would be placed in Mr. Camper's folder and your folder. Your letter indicating the charges are retracted has not been received in this office as you had promised.

Your explanation of your accusations regarding moral conduct is quite unique. However, you and other teachers at your school are discerning people and if situations arise which causes unfriendliness to a point of not speaking to each other, it is felt that as professional people, you can surely talk these situations over and straighten out your difficulties.

We talked at some length to you about problems at the school and the fact that Mr. Camper had some twenty-six individuals to work with, that you were one of them and it took the cooperation of all to do this. You indicated that you would try to work together for the good of the school.

We feel that your letter with general innuendoes and accusations which were not substantiated is a malicious thing and one in which you are cautioned about. It is a matter which Mr. Camper must take into consideration in his dealings with you. It is our sincere hope that you will act as a professional person from now on and conduct yourself accordingly. Unless such action on your part is forth coming it will be necessary to take steps to see that a professional attitude is established at Greasewood Boarding School.

Carson V. Ryan,
Subagency School Superintendent

CVRyan:dad:1-23-62

cc: Mr. Hayward Camper, Principal
    Area Personnel

**UNITED STATES
DEPARTMENT OF THE INTERIOR**
BUREAU OF INDIAN AFFAIRS
Navajo Agency
Fort Defiance Subagency
Fort Defiance, Arizona

January 22, 1962

Administratively Restricted

Mr. Noah S. Coleman, Jr.
Greasewood Boarding School
Ganado, Arizona

Through: Mr. Hayward Camper,
Principal

Dear Mr. Coleman:

Through: Mr. Hayward Camper,
Principal

Dear Mr. Coleman:

Fort De: competent i a   a whole.
iance, Nav;   1975   rincipal o: cordial d;tion
                                                                         a valuabl;
         To Whom I   formed the ties, he h;nal

                         programs, but to th;   fiance Ager
                         highly recommended   ;jo Nation,
                         tion.

                                                                              ;t
                         and satisfa   Mr. Haywa;
Since Mr.f Greasewoc;meanor at   ;e asset to
Boarding duties ass;s been a c

Arizona 86504   ;d
         ;igned in   Fort Def   June 9, ;u;
June 9,
         ;tion   ;t;

97

as planned. You are further cautioned that malicious gossip is a det-
riment to the education of the Navajo children which is our first concern
in that the morale of the children depends upon the morale of the teachers.

Sincerely yours,

(signature)

Carson V. Ryan
Subagency School Superintendent

CVRyan:dad:1-22-62
cc: Mr. Hayward Camper, Principal
    Area Personnel

Because of their letter, a visit was made to my school by the
Sub-agency School Superintendent and the Acting Sub-agency
Administrative Officer. After their visit the three teachers involved
were asked that they conduct themselves in a professional manner.
Soon after that they transferred to other schools.

The building program for the large boarding school at Greasewood
was completed for the 1946 fall session. It was built for 690 students.
The academic building had 23 classrooms, a library, multi-purpose
room, preview room, school offices and a clinic for a full time
nurse. There were four large dormitories, a large kitchen and dining
room, 52 two and three bedroom houses, 20 efficiency apartments,
maintenance shop and fire station. We had a full enrollment when
school opened with fifty or more students on our bus run or within
walking distance. Employees' children rode a bus to the public
school at Ganado.

Isabell was transferred from Indian Wells to teach in one of the
classrooms now that I had two teacher supervisors and did not
directly supervise the teachers. I wish the BIA policy had been such
that my wife could have been one of my teacher supervisors. She
gave 100 percent of herself and more. In 1972 she was selected as
one of the Outstanding Teachers of America.

Though I had a large school and was responsible for everything that
happened, good or bad, it was less of a problem than the smaller
Greasewood School because I was fortunate enough to have good
and well-qualified people in charge of each department. Things at

the school went along well until about 1971 when Navajo school boards were being developed across the reservation, and there was a push to get more Navajo teachers and administrators in positions.

Whenever I had the choice of two equally qualified people and one was a Navajo, I had always hired the Navajo. This was the Navajo reservation. I was in the business of educating Navajo children. I wanted them to have a good role model around them.

For jobs that did not require a degree or special training, I would go to the chapter house and work with the chapter officers in getting someone. I was careful and tried to spread the jobs around so they would not all go to chapter officers' families or friends. I did this by going to chapter meetings, telling members about the job and what training or work experience was needed to fill it. Those interested in working at the school could then come by the school for an interview. Then I would have them meet with the supervisor of the department they were to work in. For a while the school board worked with me meeting with school supervisors and those interested in working at the school.

Then, the school board president, Mr. Edward Tsosie decided he was going to decide who worked at the school and he began trying to select all of his friends and family members. I would be with the school board, the department head going over and discussing those we had interviewed and thought best for the job. My department head and I would agree on a certain person and most of the time we had all or most of the board members in agreement except the president. I would call the school superintendent, discuss the job and the selection with him. He would agree with me then the president of the school board would ask to speak to the superintendent, who was a Navajo. Mr. Tsosie would talk in Navajo so I never knew what was said. The superintendent, Dr. Sam Billison would ask to talk to me again. He would tell me the person I wanted for the job may be the best, but it was not the school board president's wish and I need to work and get along with him and hire the person he wanted.

I struggled with the hiring problem and thought I was making some improvement when at the end of the 1947 school year I received a plate from the school board that read, "In Appreciation For Outstanding Service as Principal 1973-1974". I did not understand why it was given to me. The school board president and I did not have the best of a school year. He had even told me the school needed a Navajo principal that could talk to the parents in their own language. That using an interpreter neither the parents or I got the true meaning of what was said.

I thanked the board for the plate went to Fort Defiance to show my supervisor. I walked into Dr. Billison's office with plate in hand. "You have been telling me I don't work hard enough to get along with my school board. Look what they gave me!" "Hayward, you don't know what that is? That is your going away present. They want you to leave and the 1973-1974 school year to be your last," he said.

Well, that took the wind out of my sails. I thought foolish me. He is right. I stayed another year and retired in June 1975.

I was in my mid fifties. Through the working years I had been going most summers to summer school. My certification for teaching or administration for New Mexico or Arizona I could readily obtain. There had been many improvements in race relations since I first went on the reservation. I could go to any restaurant, sit down and eat. I could stay in any hotel. Black people were being hired in most public schools and some even as principals and superintendents. The ghost of Mc Nary surely would not come back to haunt me after all of these years.

I wanted to live in a small town like Winslow, Arizona. You could walk where you wanted to go. There would be no need for a car or public transportation. When I was on the reservation I went to Winslow often and had friends there. I thought I could get a job in the public school system or maybe something in Flagstaff. However, Winslow wasn't to be. Isabell wanted to live in Albuquerque, New Mexico.

She was more of an active person than me and wanted to be involved in church, clubs and community work. After years on the reservation she was deserving of something she wanted so Albuquerque it was. Also being in a larger city my job chances should be better.

This country and the world have lost a great deal by not treating everyone equally. We use reasons such as race, wealth, family background, profession, sex, and other reasons to discriminate. If we did treat every person the same there would be no wars or threats of war. There would be no population where people were hungry or without proper housing or health care. There would be no need for welfare, jails, etc. The money and energy we use fighting wars and preparing to fight could be used to ensure every person had a happy and productive life. Why can't we see this? We are said to be the most intelligent of all the animals on earth yet I fear the end result of the way we are going will end with us destroying the world and everything in it. As has been said many times, "Oh, what fools we mortals be."

At 55 years old, health not bad, a little high blood pressure, a premature retirement, I felt maybe I should have hung in there a little longer at Greasewood and made them retire me if they really wanted me out. I could have had a couple more years of work. We could live on my retirement, but not very well. Oh, well, what's done is done.

CHAPTER 13

I went to the Albuquerque education office expecting with my education and experience that I would have no trouble getting a job. Really, I felt my experience supervising such a large boarding school compared with being superintendent of a small school district. They would be lucky getting me. Well, was I in for a surprise. I was told my only chance of getting a job was as a teacher in one of the schools and the principals at the schools did the hiring. I would have to visit the schools and talk to the principals. This didn't go well with me.

I didn't know any principals or which school had vacancies or where the schools were located. I don't remember what I said, but the office staff sent me to an office down the hall to talk to the equal employment officer. He not only was black, but had worked a few years on the reservation. Not long enough for a retirement, but maybe four or five years. I met him once at some workshop. He was no help so I couldn't figure out why I was sent to see him except maybe to get me out of their office. Anyway, I figured I was not going to be getting a job in the Albuquerque school system any time soon, so I went down town to the city's employment office.

I felt I was getting the same old run around that I didn't expect now. Things were suppose to be different and I was sure that had I been white with my experience in education, certification in administration and teaching and enough education beyond a master's for an educational specialist degree, they would not have let me out of the education office without an offer.

I filled out some papers at the employment office and was told if I did not have a job in a given amount of time I would be eligible for an unemployment check. I asked them how could that be when I had just retired from government service and would be receiving a retirement check. They told me that made no difference, I was looking for a job and didn't have one. This didn't sound right, but I wasn't going to argue about it.

That Sunday I was looking at the want ads in the newspaper and saw where a math teacher was needed at the New Mexico Girls school. This was not a public school, but a school under the department of corrections. I was really excited. I had majored in math many years ago, but never had the opportunity to teach high school mathematics. I would have to do some brushing up, but I could handle it.

I walked into the principal's office with my certificate and letters of recommendation feeling I had a job for sure. The principal, Mr. Gordon looked over my papers and then said, "We can't hire you. You're from out of state. You need to be here a year before we could consider you." I couldn't believe this. I told him I had a New Mexico certification. "I know and that is good, but you have not been in the state a year. You lived in Arizona. I have to give first consideration to New Mexicans," he said.

I left feeling really down. I then decided to wait a few weeks and if I didn't get anything in one of the schools, I would take a dishwashing job until something better came along. I had seen several signs where dishwashers were needed. I also was thinking the Girls' School may not be able to get a math teacher. The pay was very low, much lower than public school and teachers were on duty year round. Since Isabell and I were retired from government service I could afford to work at the low pay.

Yes, it did happen. The principal at the Girls' School was not able to get anyone or the person he had in mind decided not to take it. A week had passed and he called to see if I was still interested in the job. I was hired. I was now on cloud nine. I went to the employment office and told them I had a job and to take my name off their list. They were surprised and more so when I told them I would be teaching math at the New Mexico Girls' School. They had really expected me not to be able to find a job and have to receive unemployment.

When I started working, the school was going through troubling times. There was a staff of eleven and they were very unhappy. A few of them talked about striking, but never did. The turnover, was high.

There were cottages for the girls, one for girls in trouble with the law and another for girls on welfare. They did their best to keep the girls separated. The delinquent girls did not have any classes or activities with the welfare girls. I never have understood why the welfare girls were not housed in a building off the compound and going to public schools in the city. I also thought the teachers should be public school teachers and there would not be the morale problem of lower pay and not having summers off.

It was the teachers' responsibility to take each child at the grade level she was and continue her education so when she went back to public school no time was lost. However, there were some courses that we didn't teach. A number of girls in trouble with the law did not have serious offenses. Those who were guilty of truancy from school, run-a-ways, parents unable to control them, etc. were usually back in their regular school after three months and several trips to court where something was worked out.

We gave some of the older girls GED tests when they were prepared.

I was at the Girls School for little more than a year when the principal left. The teachers asked me to consider taking the job since I had been a principal on the reservation. I thought about it but decided not to. I told them, "No way." I was happy in the classroom teaching math. I had a job I enjoyed and did not want the headaches that came with being an administrator.

After a few months the superintendent called me to his office and asked me if I would consider taking the principal job. He had looked over my application for employment and with my background and experience felt I would be perfect for the job. I told him I wasn't sure I wanted the job and working in the correction department would be much different than my work with the BIA. He asked me to think about it for a week and let him know. He also said if I took the position and discovered I didn't want it I could go back to the classroom. I knew I was qualified for the job, but I also realized that the salary, like the teacher salary, was so much lower than principals in public school, they had a hard time getting and keeping people. I decided to take it.

The school building was small. The one school office was shared by the principal and school secretary. She was very efficient and had been in the position for years. She knew what records to keep and what reports to go out. When the principal was absent, she was the acting principal. Not having a teacher supervisor or a vice principal, she was a good person to have around. However, she was a smoker. The principal before me was also a smoker so the school office was always full of smoke. The principal smokes so much he had been nicknamed "Smoky".

The children at school were given two smoke breaks a day, one in the morning and one in the afternoon. The teachers who smoked would go with the smoking group and they would smoke away. The teachers who didn't smoke would be with the nonsmokers. Teachers had the habit of telling students who were giving them trouble in class, they would take away their smoke break if they didn't get their act together.

My first action as principal was to stop the smoke breaks at school. They had smoke breaks at the cottages over which I had no jurisdiction. If I had, I would have stopped that also, but the cottage was going to be the only place they could smoke. Now over 25 years later there is no smoking on campus for students or staff.

My teachers who smoked were angry they didn't have a break and my teachers that didn't smoke were angry because they didn't have the break to take away when children were not behaving. Also, one of the psychiatrists was agreeing with the teachers saying it was a stupid move. These children had smoked most of their lives and taking that away from them would cause all sorts of behavior problems. The teachers that wanted me to apply for the principal job now had second thoughts. I was too bossy. The job had gone to my head.

They got together and went to the superintendent. Now I wished I had talked it over with him before I did it, but that was too late now. It wasn't too late, however, to tell him why I made the change. I talked about the health issue and that some of the girls as young as ten and twelve who had no business even thinking about smoking. Many of them had developed the habit because they were there. He agreed with me and for a while I thought he would stop the smoking in the cottages, but he didn't.

I told the teachers if they had behavior problems with any student to use their intercom to the office and someone would be in their classroom right away to remove the student. We had a number of problems at first, but after a time things returned to normal and we had less problems than we did when we had the smoke break.

Now that I had the smoking of the children taken care of I asked my secretary if she would please go outside to smoke. She said, "Hell no! I am not going outside to smoke. If the smoke bothers you, then you move your desk outside or in the hall. I'm not going anywhere."

I tried, really tried for several weeks to make it work in the same office with my secretary, and I think she did slow down a little on her smoking, but in the end I could not handle it. The building had a small auditorium. I asked maintenance to use a corner and block it off for an office. I told her and others I sometimes had private matters to talk about with staff and could not do it with an open office.

My secretary laughed and said, "No, Mr. Camper moved out to get away from my smoke." I didn't care what was thought or said, my smoke problem had been solved and my secretary and I had a much better working relationship.

After several years on the job a decision was made to build a larger institution, and since the Boys' School at Springer was always over-crowded, to build it large enough to house boys also. When the building program was completed we had five large new cottages, three for boys and two for girls. We also had a library, offices for counselors and administration, a large gym with a weight room, swimming pool and a basketball area. The name changed to Youth Diagnostic and Development Center (YDDC). My office was separated from my secretaries - I now had two. I had a vice principal who also had an office. There was a large kitchen and dining room, administration building with offices and a clinic for a nurse.

I felt they should have enlarged the boys school at Springer or build another institution somewhere else for the boys. We had enough problems with the girls without adding more with boys.

It took awhile for the population to build up, but build up it did. When it was low we did a wonderful job with the children, but in time the courts were sending us so many children our programs were not as effective as they could have been. We were still under the Department of Corrections and under that umbrella had an educator who had regular meetings with the principals of the various institutions to discuss ways to improve the educational programs. We did not meet at one institution, but each meeting would be at a different institution so we could observe other operations and get ideas.

Meeting at the penitentiaries and especially the one in Santa Fe, I saw so many young men who had been at YDDC. They called out from their prison cell as I passed, "Hello, Mr. Camper." Too many young people being discharged from the youth facilities were ending up in adult prison. A great deal of this was because of over-crowding and not being able to give the children the individual attention needed. We also needed more community programs in which to grow and develop.

Many years later the state put the youth facilities under the department of New Mexico Youth Authority, but they needed to do more than change the name.

I remember a young lady in my office about to be released and I was looking over her grades, which were very good. I told her what a bright future she could have if she stayed in school and away from drugs. She had been here six months without drugs and she should just continue to stay away from drugs when she got out. "Oh, Mr. Camper, you just don't know. Out there people are saying, here, here! They are all around using and giving you drugs," she said.

I told her I had never had anyone come up to me and insist I take it. She laughed and said they wouldn't do that to me. Then she looked at my arms. I had a short sleeve shirt on and had spots on my arm that I had received years before in Los Angeles frying doughnuts. "Oh! Mr. Camper," she said, "You do it too." I was really embarrassed. I told her I didn't do drugs – not at all. Then I tried to explain to her how I got the marks on my arms. I don't know if she believed me or not. I then began to wonder how many of the other students had noticed the marks on my arm and thought I was doing drugs or had done them.

After this occurrence I always wore long sleeve shirts. Working at YDDC I saw many youngsters whose family members had been responsible for their start with drugs. Therefore, I could understand them thinking that most people use them. What chance does a child have in an environment where a mother is so strung out on drugs she will put her daughter on the street to get money for her habit.

I have always believed that a person has a choice of not using drugs even if they get caught up in the habit. Several times in my young life I thought about trying it and stopping so I would know, but I never was brave enough. I read about people receiving treatment and doing their best to quit the drug habit. It seems a few do, but a very few. I see this as our biggest problem today. The prisons are filled with more people because of a drug problem than for any other reason. People kill, rob and will do anything for drugs. If we would think of it as a medical problem before a person turns to crime to take care of it, we perhaps would make more progress in solving the problem.

Locking people up as we have been doing for years, hasn't abated the problem. It just seems to get worse. The money spent for incarceration could be better used for treatment centers, job training, quality education, and more social workers. Currently, social workers have so many clients they can't properly take care of any of them. People need to feel they are useful and have something to live for. Communities should not be allowed to deteriorate and become run-down for any reason. All should be well-kept so children can have a healthy environment to live in. Don't say we can't afford it. The reality is we can't afford not to.

How can we expect to lock up a youngster then throw him or her back in the same jungle of distress and expect that person to live a happy and productive life. Yes, a few do make it in spite of the odds, but with the proper help and environment many more would succeed.

The superintendent who hired me as principal at YDDC took the job of warden at one of the prisons and later became secretary of corrections for the State of New Mexico. The new superintendent at YDDC and I did not have the same trust and working relations as the one who hired me. He said I was doing a good job and gave me a good evaluation, but we did not have the same respect for each other. He was having trouble finding and keeping a person in the deputy superintendent position. I had a vice principal whom I had first hired as a physical education teacher for the girls. Observing how effective she was working with students and staff when my vice principal position became vacant asked her if she would be interested in taking it. She said she would. She accepted the position and together we ran a successful educational program.

The superintendent asked me if I thought my vice principal would make a good deputy. I told him sure she would. I had worked with her for years and knew should do well in any position and I saw a move to deputy as a promotion for her which she deserved. I did not want to lose her, but would never stand in her way for a promotion. I also had very able teaching staff to promote in her position.

The change was made. My vice principal became a deputy and one of my teachers became my vice principal. For several years this arrangement worked well considering our crowded conditions. At times we made an early release of a youngster because of the population increase. The judges did try to work with us, but because of the lack of community programs there was little they could do.

The boys school at Springer and YDDC had the same staffing pattern. The school principal was under the direct supervision of the superintendent. The cottage supervisors were under the direct supervision of the deputy, but all of us got together at staff meetings and under the guidance of the superintendent worked out what we thought was best for our population.

After my vice principal had been in her new position of deputy for several years the superintendent said he was changing our staffing pattern and putting the school principal under the direct supervision of the deputy.

I was not particularly thrilled about this decision. We had a good working relationship the way things were. She at the regular staff meeting would sometimes make suggestions she thought would improve the school program and I would consider them. Some I saw as good and used them, other I didn't and I would explain why I didn't think it was best for the school program. The superintendent, however, always had the final say. This had been the arrangement for years and I saw no need to change it.

I met with the superintendent and asked him why he was changing the staffing pattern and putting me under the supervision of the deputy. He mentioned her years working at the school and her background in education. I was twice her age and had that much more experience in education so that didn't help me understand the change. I asked the superintendent if there was something I had done that he did not agree with. He told me I was doing a good job.

I started thinking, some people don't realize it, but you do slow down with age. I was 55 years old when I started working at YDDC. I had been there for 15 years. I had at times had teachers in their late fifties or sixties and they just didn't have the energy my younger teachers had. I never fired any of them, but was always happy to help them with their retirement papers or transfer to another school. Maybe it was my time and I was not doing as well as I thought.

Oh, for a gift from God the giver to see ourselves as others see us. Let the superintendent or his deputy be honest and point out my weaknesses as they saw them. No, I cannot work with the feeling I am not producing as I should. I would like to do another five years. That would give me twenty years. No, I will give it to them and get another job. What am I thinking about? Another job? Who's going to hire me at my age? I wouldn't.

Hayward, make up your mind. What are you going to do? Hang on for another five years or give it them? With all the added pressures of the job, is it worth it? I'm going to retire. In June of 1990 I retired from YDDC.

Hayward J. Camper

Fort Defiance Agency
Fort Defiance, Navajo Nation, Arizona 86504

June 9, 1975

To Whom It May Concern:

Since Mr. Camper assumed his duties as Principal of Greasewood
Boarding School, he has consistently performed the duties assigned in
a highly competent and satisfactory manner. He has maintained a
pleasant, cordial demeanor at all times. By diligent application
of his duties, he has been a credit, not only to the educational
programs, but to the Agency as a whole. Mr. Hayward Camper is
highly recommended and will be a valuable asset to your organiza-
tion.

Sincerely yours,

Agency Superintendent

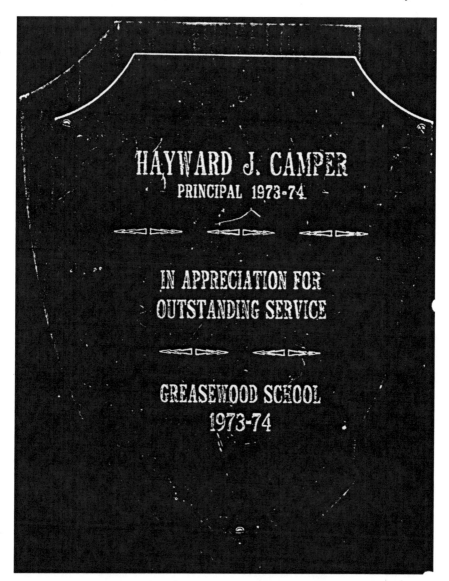

HAYWARD J. CAMPER
PRINCIPAL 1973-74

IN APPRECIATION FOR
OUTSTANDING SERVICE

GREASEWOOD SCHOOL
1973-74

Fort Defiance Agency
Fort Defiance, Navajo Nation, Arizona 86504

July 24, 1975

Mrs. Helen Westcott
State of New Mexico
State Department of Education
Education Building
Santa Fe, New Mexico 87503

Re: P 89993

Dear Mrs. Westcott:

This is to give verification that Mr. Hayward Camper, former employee at the Fort Defiance Agency since May 13, 1943 and now retired as of June 27, 1975, has been in continuous contact with Education. Your request that confirmation be given as to his teaching within the past three years is confirmed. In his role as principal in an isolated area he has been required to substitute in all the grades at his school, kindergarten through 8th., with an enrollment of 550. He has also been required to put on special teaching workshops for this agency and been required to lead or attend these meetings, as well as, assist all new teachers in his school and planned orientation workshops for teachers.

If further verification is required as to the exact number of days he was in the classroom during the past three years I will forward it upon request as it will require research.

Sincerely yours,

Ernest E. Ingraham
Acting School Superintendent

7/25/75:EEIngraham:rc

cc: Chrono
     Subject
     N36 20

THE NAVAJO NATION
WINDOW ROCK, ARIZONA 86515

PETER MacDONALD
CHAIRMAN

Mr. Haywood Camper
P.O. Box 16056
Albuquerque, New Mexico   87003

Dear Mr. Camper:

Navajo Nation Education Day has been proclaimed
for October 24, 1975. It is with great pleasure that
I, as Chairman of the Navajo Tribal Council and as a
representative of the Navajo people, recognize you on
this Second Annual Navajo Nation Education Day for your
outstanding contribution to the education and development of Navajo children.

You will be honored on Navajo Nation Education
Day at the Navajo Civic Center in Window Rock, Arizona
on October 24, 1975, for your dedicated services.

Sincerely,

PETER MACDONALD
Chairman
Navajo Tribal Council

Hayward J. Camper

Facilities for young law

By Daniel Gibson

Outside the chain-link fence a school bus rolls by, its kids crowding at the windows, yelling, the boys teasing the girls. They're on their way to swim at a city pool after school, and then home to their families.

Inside the fence there are more than 100 youths, too.

But these youths don't ride school buses, they don't go to public pools, and they don't go home to their families at the end of their school day. They're a breed apart — children behind the wire of a penal institution.

The practice of isolating boys and girls in penal institutions may be one of the saddest condemnations of modern society. It's said that today's delinquents often become tomorrow's hardcore criminals in such institutions.

In the wake of the disaster at the New Mexico state penitentiary, determining the condition of institutions for young law offenders takes on a sharp new focus.

Located on a barren hillside plot of 80 acres between Edith and Frontage Road NW in Albuquerque is one such

---

"If this place doesn't undergo a major renovation within the next five years, we might as well close it down."

---

institution for young law breakers — the combined facilities of the Youth Diagnostic Center (YDC) and the New Mexico Girl's Home.

How does the facility measure up? The News spent a day touring the institution and came away with a list of good and bad points.

• **Population:**

When YDC was created in 1972 by a court order, it recommended to juvenile judges possible courses of punitive action concerning specific girls. This role was expanded to include boys in 1974 when Springer became too crowded to carry out this function. The result has been an occasional overcrowding of YDC and the Girl's Home. Eloy Mondragon, superintendent since '74, says the facility is inadequate for its current functions. The facility is licensed for a maximum of 108 youths, but currently houses 115. There are nearly twice as many boys as girls.

• **Food:**

— it should be the other way around. Our budget — $1.539 million this year — is only enough to run our basic programs." The legislators did grant the facility an extra chunk of money this year to work on upgrading the facilities — $192,000 for a planning study. However, already pinned on Mondragon's office wall are the architectural plans for a brand new center — designed by the Fernando and Trujillo firm to the recommendations of Mondragon and his staff.

Says Mondragon, "We have buildings here going back to 1919, and others built by the WPA in the 30s." The current teaching facilities, Foothill School, have their offices and several classrooms located adjacent to the gym. All winter, lessons must be conducted to the pounding of balls and feet on the gym floor. Mondragon says there are serious heating and cooling problems with the classes as well.

As for the living quarters, Mondragon points out that they were built to isolate the kids from each other. He would like to see cottages built with an emphasis on promoting group interaction through the use of more open space and fewer walls.

The plans on Mondragon's wall call for construction in three phases, beginning with six new classrooms, a gym and pool. In additional phases, he'd like to see a new cafeteria and auditorium, then a chapel, six new cottages, and an administrative center. In the final phase, he envisions a new maintenance center, diagnostic workshops and facilities for technical training. All this, though, depends on funding from the Legislature. Acquiring the funds remains perhaps the facility's number one problem.

Mondragon puts it this way, "I'd like to see a real juvenile system developed. Now, it's fragmented. Planning is done on a crisis basis ... We need to be completely separated from the adult program."

Despite lack of direction and support from the state, the YDC program and the Girl's Home have many positive qualities.

• **Education diagnostics:**

When a youth is admitted to the center, he or she is tested for learning disabilities. The educational diagnostician, Dr. Nicholas Abeyta, has found an interesting link among many of the youths there — a high percentage have some sort of learning disability. He says, "There's a large correlation between

---

"School achievement is

---

they don't fit into a mold, they are left behind and feel they aren't wanted. The majority of the kids that appear here aren't in school at the time of arrest." The Foothill School is accredited with the state board of education and its teacher certified.

• **Medical care:**

Says the full-time nurse at the center, eight-year employee Arlene J. Olson, "In general, students are medically neglected before they are sent to us; especially in dental care." She says the most common medical problem the incoming youths have is the sniffing of paint and other solvents, a trend she says is decreasing. Head psychologist Richard Rodriguez, however, notes, "The younger the kids are, the more they seem to be into inhalant abuse." Other youth medical problems receiving a lot of attention at the center are alcohol abuse and VD. A study just completed at the center found over 60 percent of the boys and 70 percent of the girls use alcohol, and so the center is providing counseling in alcohol use.

Says Olson, "The days when I used to spot a lot of serum hepatitis (from shooting) are over, and the VD among women is decreasing, too. They're more careful today. And, I can spot the sniffers — they're always thin. I get them on vitamins to stimulate their appetite again." The center has a doctor on call 24 hours a day.

• **Staff awareness and education:**

To have a responsive staff rather than one blindly bent on discipline and authority, one that rules out of respect and not with an iron fist has been a goal of Mondragon's, and it's largely succeeded.

He says, "All my staff here has a pretty high education level, including several with degrees in corrections training and many others with other degrees." The staff, in speaking with The News, displayed a sensitivity and recognition of the special problems their clients face.

"School life for many of these kids is a very non-positive experience", says Rodriguez. "School achievement is a common problem among them. The biggest problem we have with them is their low self-esteem — a failure identity. Their drug abuse is a way of coping with this failure identity."

• **Punishment:**

Punishment policy is a far cry from that of "The Big House". Mondragon says, "We try and use positive reinforcement rather than a punitive policy. We give out positive and negative behavior

---

116

NAVAJO NATION EDUCATION DAY

OCTOBER 24, 1975

WINDOW ROCK CIVIC CENTER
WINDOW ROCK, ARIZONA

SPONSORED BY: NAVAJO DIVISION OF EDUCATION

HONOREES

1. SENATOR ARTHUR HUBBARD, Arizona State Senate
2. SENATOR TOM LEE, New Mexico State Senate
3. REPRESENTATIVE BENJAMIN HANLEY, Arizona House of Representative
4. REPRESENTATIVE DANIEL PEACHES, Arizona House of Representative
5. REPRESENTATIVE LEO WATCHMAN, New Mexico House of Representative
6. DR. TAYLOR McKENZIE, Navajo Health Authority
7. DR. SAMUEL BILLISON, Agency School Supt., Ft. Defiance, Agency
8. DR. FRED YOUNG, Los Alamos Scientific Lab.
9. DR. BAHE BILLIE, NAPI, Farmington, New Mexico
10. DR. ROBERT NORRIS, University of Arizona, Tucson, Arizona
11. DR. LLOYD HOUSE, BIA, Window Rock, Arizona
12. DR. GEORGE LEE, Southwest Indian Mission, Holbrook, Arizona
13. MR. ROSS HOSKIE, Mexican Hat Elem., Mexican Hat, Utah
14. MS. KATHRYN P. ARVISO, Ft. Lewis College, Durango, Colo.
15. MR. SAM HARRISON, Teec Nos Pos Brdg. School, Teec Nos Pos, Ariz.
16. MS. JEAN COMBS, Chinle Brdg. School, Chinle, Arizona
17. MR. STANLEY VAN KEUREN, Window Rock, Public School
18. MR. ROBERT E. KARLIN, Central Consolidated School
19. SISTER MARIJANE RYAN, St. Michaels Special Education
20. MS. LISBETH EUBANK, (Retired BIA) Scottsdale, Arizona
21. MS. EVA BENALLY Navajo Community College, Shiprock, N.M.
22. DR. WILLARD BASS, Southwest Research Associates, Albuquerque, N.M.
23. MS. ANITA PFIEFFER, University of New Mexico, Albuquerque, N.M.
24. MS. MARIE GRIMES, Puerco Elementary School, Sanders, Arizona
25. MS. INA MAE ANCE, Crownpoint Brdg. School, Crownpoint, N.M.
26. MS. HILDEGARD THOMPSON, (Retired BIA), Louisville, Kentucky
27. MS. REBECCA DOTSON, Chinle Agency Supt., Chinle, Arizona
28. MS. FARLEE SPELL, (Retired BIA), Carson City, Nevada
29. MR. KENNETH BENALLY, Nenahnezad Brdg. School, Fruitland, N.M.
30. SISTER GLORIA DAVIS, St. Michaels School, St. Michaels, Arizona
31. MR. CLEVELAND MILLER, Chinle Brdg. School, Chinle, Arizona
32. MR. HAYWOOD CAMPER, (Retired BIA), Albuquerque, N.M.
33. MR. LEON A. ASHLEY, Teec Nos Pos Brdg. School, Teec Nos Pos, Ariz.

MORNING SESSION

11:00 a.m. MISTRESS OF CEREMONY: JOY HANLEY

9:30 a.m. REGISTRATION AND COFFEE

10:30 a.m. INVOCATION: MR. STEWART ETCITTY

INTRODUCTION:

WELCOME ADDRESS:
DILLON PLATERO, Director
Navajo Division of Education

FEATURE SPEAKER:
PETER MacDONALD, Chairman
Navajo Tribal Council

PRESENTATION OF AWARDS TO HONOREES:

DR. FRED YOUNG
DR. LLOYD HOUSE
DR. GEORGE LEE
DR. SAMUEL BILLISON
DR. BAHE BILLIE
DR. ROBERT NORRIS
DR. TAYLOR McKENZIE

SENATOR ARTHUR HUBBARD
SENATOR TOM LEE
REPRESENTATIVE BENJAMIN HANLEY
REPRESENTATIVE DANIEL PEACHES
REPRESENTATIVE LEO WATCHMAN

GUEST SPEAKER:
DR. WILLIAM BUD DAVIS, President
University of New Mexico
Albuquerque, New Mexico

12:00 NOON LUNCH

AFTERNOON SESSION

1:30 p.m. MASTER OF CEREMONY MR. JACK JACKSON

GENERAL SESSION

ENTERTAINMENT:
CHILD DEVELOPMENT PROGRAM
Ft. Defiance, Arizona

GUEST SPEAKER:
DR. HELEN SCHIERBECK, Chairman
Task Force on Indian Education
American Indian Policy Review Commission

PRESENTATION OF AWARDS TO HONOREES:
Presentation of Awards -
MR. ANTHONY LINCOLN - BIA Area Director

MR. ROSS HOSKIE
MR. SAM HARRISON
MR. STANLEY VAN KEUREN
SISTER MARIJANE RYAN
MS. ANITA PFIEFFER
MS. INA MAE ANCE
MS. REBECCA DOTSON
MR. KENNETH BENALLY
SISTER GLORIA DAVIS
MS. HILDEGARD THOMPSON

MS. KATHRYN ARVISO
MS. JEAN COMBS
MR. ROBERT E. KARLIN
MS. LIZBETH EUBANK
DR. WILLARD BASS
MS. MARIE GRIMES
MS. CLEVELAND MILLER
MS. FARLEE SPELL
MR. LEO ASHLEY
MR. HAYWOOD CAMPER

CLOSING REMARKS:
ROBERT BILLIE, Chairman
Education Committee
Navajo Tribal Council

BENEDICTION:
MARIE HARDY, Counselor
Navajo Division of Education

3:30 p.m. ADJOURNMENT:

118

MEMORANDUM   DECEMBER 23, 1976

TO: ALL AREAS

FROM: ELOY MONDRAGON, SUPERINTENDENT
           MARY KARNES, DEPUTY SUPERINTENDENT

SUBJECT: SCHOOL PRINCIPAL

Mr. Hayward Camper has been appointed Principal of Foothill
High School at New Mexico Youth Diagnostic Center. He will
begin his duties in that position on Monday, December 27, 1976.
Please refer all questions about the school program to him.

Eloy Mondragon
Eloy Mondragon
Superintendent

Mary Karnes
Mary Karnes
Deputy Superintendent

EM:MK:jr

PART IV

CHAPTER 14

It wasn't long before I had a job, teaching math at the Heights Psychiatric Hospital. Children were in the hospital until released by their doctors and returned to their regular school. The classes were small and most of the time the children worked well in class. When there was a problem there was always staff available to take care of it. I was happy with this job and it wasn't far from where I lived.

Sometime in 1993 I went to Lovelace for my regular six-month check up. My doctor gave me the regular exam, told me I was fine and he would see me in six months. It was just a week before that I read an article about a blood test for prostate cancer. As I was getting ready to leave the doctor's office I asked him about it. At first he said I did not need it, I was fine. Then as I was going out the door he stopped me and said it would be a good idea to have the blood test. There was a greater chance for cancer in my race than the white race. He said he had irritated the area so he could not do the test now, but he scheduled me to come back in a week. After a week I went back and they took some blood.

I went back to work. Several weeks passed. I had heard nothing so I thought everything was all right. Then about the third week they called me in to say I had a high prostate specific antigen (PSA) and they needed to take a biopsy. About a week after the biopsy my doctor called me back to his office to say I had cancer and should have an operation. Isabell was with me and angry that I had to ask about the blood test. If it had been done regularly they could have prevented the cancer sooner. She told the doctor we were going to the University Hospital for the operation and to send my medical records there. My doctor didn't like this and looked at me and asked if I was sure that was what I wanted to do. I told him yes, but it really didn't matter to me.

I felt any doctor could remove the cancer, but my daughter who was a nurse had told us to get a doctor who had done a number of operations and since the University Hospital was a cancer hospital my wife thought they would have done more operations than the Lovelace Hospital.

We were told my medical records would be sent to the University Hospital. They never were sent, so my wife went to the office at Lovelace, got them and took them to the University Hospital.

The doctors at University Hospital talked about different ways to treat the cancer, but after talking with them, we thought an operation was best. Cut it **out!** I thought that would be the end of it. I don't think the doctors were really saying this, but that is the way I was hearing it. After the removal of the prostate I was scheduled to come back in six months for a check up. I didn't understand then what I know now. Once you have cancer you can do numerous things to make its presence disappear, but there is always the possibility that it will pop up again.

Once I healed from the operation I went back to Heights Psychiatric Hospital to see about my job. They had someone working in my position and they did not have a vacancy. Though I wasn't given sick leave I left with the feeling I would be able to return there for work after my operation. I decided to do some volunteer work and hang loose until something was available. I did volunteer work at Lovelace's Journal Center site. I gave patients information for location to doctors' offices, I got wheel chairs if needed, or assisted patients in any way I could.

I did this for six months, checking often at Heights to see if they had a position for me. At first I thought they may, but after a time I decided they weren't going to have anything. Also they were cutting back and phasing out their education program.

When I returned to the doctor for my six-month checkup I was informed my cancer was active again. The doctor discussed various treatments available to me, but the one that was of interest to me was the removal of the testicles. The doctor said the cancer cells live on what the testicles secrete. Also he said removal of the testicles was a minor operation and I would not have to stay in the hospital. My thought was take away the testicles and the cancer cells would have no food. They would have to die and stay gone.

After the operation I went home, but things did not go right for me. I had a great deal of swelling and much pain, so my wife took me back to the hospital where I spent the night. My doctor again told me I would need to come in every six months for a check up. Now it has been over 13 years since this episode. One time there was upward movement of my PSA and my doctor checked me every three months. I am now back to every six months. When I start feeling that the cancer will not be back my doctor does something to make me realize that just isn't so. The last time, he was going through the folder with the paperwork of all my treatment and said, "Let me see, that has been 12 years and you are still cancer free. That is very unusual." I wanted to tell him I wasn't expecting cancer to kill me no matter how many years I live.

I gave up volunteer work and got a job as a substitute in the Albuquerque Public School System. Years ago they would not hire me as a regular teacher, but now they would let me be a substitute. Maybe they would hire me now as a teacher, But I wasn't interested. At first I enjoyed working, going to schools all over the city. The staff, the children and everything was good. Then I got tired of traveling all over the city and wanted to be able to go to one school all the time. Since the place I retired from (YDDC) needed substitutes and the superintendent who was there when I retired was gone I decided to do sub work there.

It was strange going back to YDDC. They had built another unit for high-risk boys. These boys did not come in contact with the YDDC students at all. Their schooling, meals, recreation, medical, everything was in their building. They did share the same superintendent, principal and vice principal, so as a sub I would work there as well as at YDDC. About one third of the staff was still there who were there when I left. One of my teachers at the time was now principal. He was happy to have me on board, however, I was under his vice principal's supervision. I had been gone for 10 years.

Most classrooms had too many children just as they had when I was there before. At Heights' the average class size was no more than 15. That was a good number to work with and more so since you had children with special problems.

Some of the children's parents at YDDC told them they remembered me working there when they were there. Isn't that sad? This was a repeated cycle and an example where money had been used to build more lockups, but not to improve conditions in the community.

Working with the boys in the new complex that had been built for boys with serious crimes was interesting. They wanted to know how many times I had been locked up and what kind of trouble I got into when I was young. When I told them I had never been locked up they told me right out, "You lie!" Most people they knew had been in and out of penal institutions, and were using and/or selling drugs. They didn't know any other life.

One of the boys asked me how old I was. When I told him he said I was lying. I couldn't be that old. I had already been accused of not telling the truth, but NOW I had the opportunity to prove I was telling the truth, so I gave him my drivers license to look at. He looked at it and in surprise turned to the class and said. "This cat really is that old." Then he gave the license to me and said "Old man, you should have dropped long ago." I told him when I got to be a hundred I would think about it.

I did substitute work at YDDC for about a year when my wife broke a bone in her foot and it was necessary for me to be at home. Now she is all right, but she didn't want me to go back. It does feel good not having to get up and go, but it also felt nice being on the job with the children, too. Oh, well, you can't have it both ways.

CHAPTER 15

Looking back I continue to believe we have lost too many young children by not giving them a chance to continue their education. Even today there are many children living in poor communities where schools are not as equipped as schools in affluent communities, so their education program is inadequate. It is imperative that all schools have adequate resources for children to succeed.

We continue to think that building more prisons and lock-up facilities is better than building better schools and communities. We prefer to spend more money for larger military forces, more firepower and deadly arsenals, newer and better ways to kill than to research and focus on eliminating sickness, hunger and poverty. We'd rather incarcerate drug addicts than wipe out the source of drugs and develop rehabilitation programs. We spend millions to find out if there is or ever was life on Mars rather than improving life on earth. Individuals still don't believe God created all men equal. There continues to be disparities among cultures and races. Our problems are many and complex, but we have many talented men and women who may one day use their creativity and intelligence to cure some of the world's ills rather than allowing society to self-destruct.

If I should come this way again, I hope I will think less of self-satisfaction and be more understanding of, and look for the good in others. I would look for more ways to help others. Also that I would appreciate that this world was not made for man alone, but for all creatures large or small. The sun, the moon, the stars, the sky, the trees, the mountains, the sea, the flowers, the grass and all creations were made for every creature to enjoy. Yesterday is gone, tomorrow never comes, but today is here forever. It is what we do today that counts. Do the best you can each hour of the day to make this world a better place for all living things.

Acknowledgements

Thanks to my wife, Isabell J. Camper for standing by me through all the rough years. And, thanks to my two daughters who helped their mother by helping with their younger brothers while their mother was in school and their father away working on the Navajo reservation. I also thank my wife for her help and suggestions in writing about our years together. It still just seems like yesterday. Time really does fly and the older you get the faster it goes.

Also, a special thanks to Mrs. Virginia P. Grant for believing I had a story to tell and taking the bits and parts, putting them together for all to read.

I know this is a bit unusual, but I wish to say it. The poem, **If**, written by Rudyard Kipling (1865-1936), a leading British English short-story writer, poet and novelist, was on our wall in Prescott and I have it on my wall today. It has been a guiding light for me through all my years, and I would like to share my source of encouragement with you.

> "If you can keep your head when all about you
> Are losing theirs and blaming it on you,
> If you can trust yourself when all men doubt you,
> But make allowance for their doubting too,
> If you can wait and not be tired by waiting,
> Or being lied about, don't deal in lies,
> Or being hated, don't give way to hating,
> And yet don't look too good, nor talk too wise:

If you can dream - - and not make dreams your master;
If you can think - - and not make thoughts your aim;
If you can meet with Triumph and Disaster
And treat those two imposters just the same,
If you can bear to hear the truth you've spoken
Twisted by knaves to make a trap for fools,
Or watch the things you gave your life to, broken,
And stoop and build 'em up with worn-out tools;

If you can make one heap of all your winnings
And risk it on one turn of pitch-and-toss,
And lose, and start again at your beginnings
And never breathe a word about your loss;
If you can force your heart and nerve and sinew
To serve your turn long after they are gone,
And so hold on when there is nothing in you
Except the Will which says to them: 'Hold on!'

If you can talk with crowds and keep your virtue,
Or walk with kings - - nor lose the common touch,
If neither foes nor loving friends can hurt you,
If all men count with you, but none too much;
If you can fill the unforgiving minute
With sixty seconds' worth of distance run - -
Yours is the Earth and everything that's in it,
And - - which is more - - you'll be a Man, my son!"

Isn't it beautiful? I never had to recite it for the many programs I
was in as a child, but I had it in my thoughts and memory through
many of my hard times.

#

We, the Editors of the
1972 Mustang!, dedicate
this book to the staff
and students of our school.

We appreciate being here
in Greasewood.

Priscilla Miles
and Staff

Greasewood Boarding School

1972

ANNUAL STAFF

EDITOR........PRISCILLA MILES

Advisor.......Mrs. M. Beaumont

Margaret John	Rebecca Nelson
Eva Mae Curley	Rose Begay
Linda Benally	Lula Nez

SCHOOL BOARD

Not Shown:
Mr. C. Yazzie

Mr. C. Begay
Mr. M. Chee

Mr. E. Tsosie,
President

Mr. A. Yazzie

PRINCIPAL

Mr. H. J. Camper

Mr. J. G. Kipp,
Supervisory Guidance
Counselor

Miss H. Zongolowicz
Student Activity Director
(Acting)

Mr. J. D. Todd
Teacher Supervisor
(Acting)

132

SPECIAL SERVICES

rs. Marcia Beaumont   Mr. J. B. Macias   Mrs. Eula Hughes   Mr. Craig Reis
Counselor   Counselor   Librarian   Recreation Spe

OFFICE STAFF

Mrs. Irene Sangster   Mrs. Judi Maestas   Mrs. Fannie Roan
Enrollment Clerk   Head Clerk   Clerk

CUSTODIAL SERVICES

Mrs. Lillian Yazzie   Mr. Edgar Bitahe

FACULTY

Mrs. T. Salabiye   Mrs. M. Bitsilly   Mrs. L. Gorman

Miss D. Cole   Mrs. R. Johnson

Mr. M. James   Mr. H. Denetso   Mrs. M. Begay

Mrs. I. Camper   Miss R. Sangster   Mrs. F. Holmes   Mrs. M. A. King

134

Mrs. M. Harvey   Mr. R. Tobey   Mr. F. Bitsilly

Miss V. Neal   Miss J. Tsosie   Mrs. P. Reisinger Mrs. M. Wor

Mr. M. Little   Mrs. P. Wigglesworth   Mrs. C. Kelley   Mr. O. For

Not Shown:

Mrs. B. Begay   Mrs. L. Mathe
Mr. I. Begay   Mr. O. Edward
Mr. T. Beyal   Mr. T. Marr
Miss M. Mahoney   Mr. R. Hartzl
Mrs. D. Denetso

Mr. M. Purifoy   Mr. D. Hundley

GUIDANCE DEPARTMENT

Mrs. M. Anthony

Mrs. E. Bitah

Mrs. L. Frank

Mr. R. Gishey

Mrs. E. James

Mrs. R. Kanuho

Mr. J. Salabiye

Mrs. B. Thomas

Mr. L. Thomas

Mrs. L. Tsosie

Mrs. P. White

Mrs. Betty Yazzie

Not Shown:

Mrs. M. Begay	Mrs. O. Poseyesva	Mrs. E. Lynch	Mr. E. Keedah
Mr. C. Kanuho	Mrs. I. Smith	Mrs. M. Sangster	Mr. J. Curley
Mr. H. Sangster	Mrs. P. Tracy	Mrs. J. Ben	Mr. L. Frank
Mrs. J. Peterson	Mrs. F. Curtis	Mrs. P. Curley	Mrs. C. Gishey
Mrs. E. Sangster	Mrs. O. James	Mrs. S. Yazzie	Mr. E. Antonio
Mrs. F. Nelson	Mrs. S. White	Mrs. H. Kaye	Mr. R. Pioche
Mrs. M. L. Begay			
Mrs. M. Bitah			

Standing (L to R): P. Kamensky
(Dentist), D. Ross (Doctor),
Wilson Yazzie
Seated (L to R) A. Bush, C. Joe,
S. Dineyazhe (RN), C. Antonio

KITCHEN

nding (L to R): D. Dalgai,
Stewart, L. Smith, W. White,
Curtis (Head Cook)
ted (L to R) L. Sangster,
Joe, F. Begay, D. Woodie,
Joseph

PLANT
MANAGEMENT

Not Shown: Andrew Ben
            Guy Yazzie

Standing: David Sangster, Rick Eustace (Foreman),
Charlie T. Yazzie; Seated: Herman Dale,
Cecil Begay, Ray Davis

HIGH SCHOOL
DAYS

Class of 1972
Eighth Grade

Kevin Becenti

Elvis Begay

Franklin J. Begay

Geraldine Begay

Jack Begay

Jimmie Begay

Jones Begay

Richard Begay, Jr.

Rose Begay

Stella Begay

Marilyn Belin

Linda Benally

Johnny Bitahe

140

Kee Bitsilly, Jr.   Yvonnie Blackgoat   Harrison Boyd   Eva Mae

Wayne Curley   Jeffery Gaddy   Kathleen Gishey

Jean Joe   Marlene Joe   Margaret John   Dennis

Ernest Kee   Angeline Lee   Evangeline Maize

Priscilla Miles   Don Frank Nelson   Rebecca Nelson   Frank Nez

Lula Nez   Gary Paul   Laura Reed

Lela Ann Roan   Edith Shorty   Marlene Shorty   Marcella Tapaha

Eugene Thompson   Wilson Tsinnijinnie   Aurelia Tyler

Casey Tyler

Bertha Willie

Daisy Yazzie

Stella Y

Randolph Yazzie

Not Shown:
Laverne McCraith

Tommy L. Yazzie

Autographs

143

Baby Pictures

144

Seventh Grade

Beverly Begay

ranklin H. Begay

Marjorie Begay

Marlene Begay

Janice

Albert Belin

Dianne Bigman

Julia Brown

Alice Ch

Edith Claw

Ethel Claw

Barbara Cummings

Geraldine

Arlene Dalgai

Sam Evans, Jr.

Howard Gishi

Peggy Gonnie

Eileen Hill

Delmar Jim

Vera Joe

Larson John

Mae Rose John

Benjamin Kee

Rosita Kee

Freddie A. Lee

Freddie H. Lee

Lorenzo Lee

Marilyn Lee

David McCraith

Cynthia Mitchell   Thomas Gishie   Larson L. Moore   Jane

Leo Roanhorse   Nancy Tabaha   Ruby Tapaha   Emmett T.

Alfred Yazzie   Grace Yazzie   Harrison Yazzie   Herbert K.

Not Shown:

Johnson Di
Jesse Gold
Edison Jim
Darrell Ya
Rosemary F
Genevieve
Vera Miles
Marcella T
Rosebell W

Leonard Yazzie   Mary Ann Yazzie   Theresa Yazzie

147

GUESS WHO ?

6th Grade

Peter Becenti, Jr.

Anderson

Carletta Begay

Frank J. Begay, Jr.

Frederick H. Begay

Ruby J.

Evelyn Belin

Elmer Benally

Patrick Bitsui

Jackso

Harlen Charley

Patterson Charley

Henderson Begay

Mary Jan

149

Betty Clah

Anita Clark

Sarah Curley

James Etsitty

Sandra Francis

Angeline Gaddy

Cheryl Gishey

Dianna Gishey

David Gishi

Grace J. Gonnie

Evelyn Hill

Albert J. Jones

Jack Keams, Jr.

Lorraine Kee

Elaine Lee

Emerson Lee

150

Hilda Lee

Linda Lee

Sharon Lee

Lora

Rita Mann

Vangeline Maize

Katherine McCraith

Priscilla

Leroy Multine

Felix Nez

Lena Nez

Marietta

Jarvis Roan

Lorenzo Roan

Joseph Roanhorse

Natisda

151

Clyde Tapaha

Marcia Tapaha

Alvin Wilson

Rose Ann Woody

Patsy Yazzie

Not Shown:

Laverne Lee
Fannie Baloo
George Chee
Lorena Tapaha
Gloria Kee
Gilbert Gonnie

Autographs

Fifth Grade

Mr. M. Little's 5th Grade Class

Mr. Theodore Marr's 5th Grade Class
(Formerly Miss Helen Zongolowicz's Class)

Fourth Grade

Mrs. Laura Mathews' 4th Grade Class

Mr. Otis Edwards' 4th Grade Class

Third Grade

Mrs. Pamela Reisinger's 3rd Grade Class

Miss Victoria Neal's 3rd Grade Class

Mr. Ray Tobey's 3rd Grade Class

Second Grade

Mrs. M. Harvey's 2nd Grade Class

Mrs. Florence Holmes' 2nd Grade Class

Mr. Isadore Begay's 2nd Grade Class

First Grade

Mrs. Isabell Camper's 1st Grade Class

Miss Donna Cole's 1st Grade Class

Mr. Mike James' 1st Grade Class

$\mathcal{B}eginners$

Miss Mary Mahoney's Beginner Class
(Formerly Mrs. Kathy K. Steele's Class)

Kindergarten

Mrs. Theresa Salabiye's Kindergarten Class

Mrs. Lorraine Gorman's Kindergarten Class

160

Mrs. Agnes Baldwin's Head Start Class

LEARNING CENTER

Miss Catherine Milke   Miss Helen Kanyid
Miss Caroline Yazzie   Mrs. Marjorie Jimmie

LIBRARIANS

MRS. HUGHES,
  Sponser
Back: R. Begay,
K. Becenti,
S. Francis

Front:
P. Becenti,
C. Gishey,
R. J. Begay

162

Student Council

Mrs. Marcia Beaumont and Mr. J. B. Macias, Advisors
PRES....R. Begay, Jr.   VICE-PRES....K. Becenti
SEC.....L. Reed   TREASURER....M. John

Newspaper Staff

Mrs. Patricia Wigglesworth, Advisor

WINONA LODGE INDIAN CLUB
Mrs. Ora James, Sponser

SUNRISE HALL INDIAN CLUB

165

Carnival

at

Greasewood

GO MUSTANGS

Miss Donna Cole, Sponser
Cheryl Gishey, Captain
Sharon Lee   Marlene Begay
Katherine McCraith   Sandra Francis

SPORTS

Coach: Mr. Craig Reisinger

Standing (L to R): P. Miles, L. Roan, G. Dale, B. Willie, R. Begay, Manager L. Nez; Seated (L-R) E. Shorty, M. John, A. Charley, G. Yazzie, D. Yazzie, M. Tapaha, B. Begay.

Standing (L-R): J. Begay, G. Paul, A. Belin, T. Yazzie, D. Nelson; Seated (L-R): F. Nez, F. Begay, L. John, J. Bitahe, H. Boyd, Manager R. Yazzie

B TEAM

ch: Mr. Harold
Denetso

Standing (L-R): Manager M. Lee, P. Willie,
L. Lewis, B. Clah, G. Gonnie; Seated (L-R)
S. Lee, M. Tapaha, N. Tapaha, M. Pete,
P. Gonnie, A. Clark

Coach: Mr. Ronald
Gishey

Standing (L-R): F. Begay, L. Yazzi
L. Roanhorse, P. Becenti; Seated (
T. Gishey, J. Begay, J. Roanhorse,
M. Yazzie, R. Nez

169

Coaches: Mr. Ronald Gishey Standing (L-R): F. Nez, J. Begay, A. Belin,
        Mr. Tom Yazzie T. Yazzie, L. John, H. Boyd; Seated (L-R):
G. Paul, T. Gishey, D. Nelson; Kneeling:
K. Becenti, J. Bitahe

Coach: Mr. Craig Standing (L-R): B. Begay, L. Benally,
    Reisinger Manager L. Nez, R. Begay, B. Willie;
Seated (L-R): G. Begay, E. Shorty,
M. John, A. Charley, P. Miles,
M. Tapaha, L. Roan

Coach: Mr. Craig
      Reisinger

Standing (L-R): D. Yazzie, B. Begay, L. Benal
Manager L. Nez, R. Begay, B. Willie; Seated
(L-R): G. Begay, E. Shorty, M. John, A. Charle
P. Miles, M. Tapaha, L. Roan

tanding (L-R): A. Belin, D. Nelson, T. Yazzie,
. Becenti, L. John, J. Begay, F. Nez; Seated
L-R): L. Roanhorse, F. J. Begay, J. Bitahe,
. Gishey, G. Paul

Coach: Mr. Ronal
            Gishey

171

Coach: Mr. Craig Reisinger

Standing (L-R): D. Yazzie, B. Begay, L. Benally, Manager L. Nez; R. Begay, B. Willie; Seated (L-R): L. Reed, E. Shorty, M. John, A. Charley, P. Miles, M. Tapaha, L. Roan

Standing(L-R): L. John, G. Paul, A. Belin, D. Nelson, T. Yazzie, J. Gaddy; Seated (L-R): K. Roanhorse, R. Paul, M. Nez, F. Begay, J. Bitahe, J. Etsitty, E. Thompson, S. Evans; Kneeling: H. Boyd, F. Nez

Coach: Mr. Tom Yazzie

Back Row: H. Nez, R. Watchman, M. Clah,
D. Blackgoat, J. Bigman, A. Shorty;
Middle Row: F. Lee, L. Moore, J. Gaddy,
D. Kee, R. Paul, T. Yazzie; Front Row:
K. Redhorse, A. Descheenie, M. Nez,
J. Etsitty, L. Lee, W. Curley, E. Chee

Sponsor: Mr. Tom
Yazzie

Sponsers:
  Mr. Leroy Thomas
  Mr. Leon Frank

Back Row: H. Multine, _____, P. Becenti,
J. Bigman, J. Bitahe, K. Becenti;
Middle Row: T. Yazzie, J. Begay, F. Nez
Front Row: H. Boyd, E. Thompson, L. John
D. Nelson, T. Gishie, G. Paul

173

SCOUTS

Sponsers: Mrs. Marcia Beaumont,
Miss Catherine Milke & Mrs. Margaret Harvey

Sponser: Mr. Craig Reisinger

Mr. J. D. Todd
Mr. C. Reising
  Leaders
Peter Becenti
Wayne Curley,
Den Chiefs

Mrs. E. Hughes &
Mrs. N. Kipp,
  Den Mothers
Harlen Charley &
Richard Begay,
  Den Chiefs

Mrs. P. Reisinger &
Mrs. P. White,
  Den Mothers
Kevin Becenti &
Casey Tyler,
  Den Chiefs

175

Examining,
The 'Tools'

EARLY CHILDHOOD EDUCATION — Looking over some audio visual 'tools' used in an early childhood education workshop at Northern Arizona University are, left, Dr. Millicent Savery, professor of education at the University of Nebraska, who is teaching the workshop; Wayne Hopper, teacher in the Prescott public schools; Lou Neil Mayfield, teacher in the Colorado Springs, Colo., public schools; Isabell Camler, Greasewood, Ariz., Indian Boarding School, and Viola Benally, Denneholso Boarding School, Ariz. The workshop deals with the role of the school in regards to the pre-schooler (pre-kindergarten, kindergarten and 1-2-3). NAU now offers a major in early childhood education.

(NAU Photo)

176

HAVING FUN
OUT DOORS

GREASEWOOD BOARDING
SCHOOL

GRADE 1

10   1971-72

GREASEWOOD SCHOOL
GANADO ARIZONA

MRS CAMPER
GRADE 1
1972-73

178

Printed in the United States
40326LVS00006B/154-183